PRAISE FOR *TEEN QUEEN TRAININ*

"From the chapters of an overwrought 1963 etiquette manual for girls, Kristine Langley Mahler has gifted us with a series of concise, insightful, and often playful texts that turn the mirror back on the contrivance of its source material. In *Teen Queen Training,* Mahler serves as a different kind of guide from the original—wise, knowing, and experienced in navigating the minefield of instruction, expectations, and limitations that American girlhood can be. 'The real problem for every unattached female,' she tells us, 'is the expectation that a kiss has value.' Mahler finds the pointed needles of language in each haystack of admonition, reminding us that the messy and problematic artifacts of our past can—and perhaps must be—inverted, subverted, and made new."
—Mary-Kim Arnold, author of *Litany for the Long Moment*

"Using subversive technique, Mahler's *Teen Queen Training* transforms the prescriptive advice of a mid-century etiquette manual about how young women are taught to be. Form meets content in these essays, where the act of crossing out becomes a critique of the very lessons meant to shape girlhood. Inventive and haunting, *Teen Queen Training* is a bold look into the possibilities of the genre."
—LaTanya McQueen, author of *And It Begins Like This*

Teen Queen Training

Essays after *The Seventeen Book of Etiquette and Entertaining*, 1963

Kristine Langley Mahler

Autofocus Books
Easton, Pennsylvania

Published by Autofocus Books
autofocusbooks.com

Essay/Literature
ISBN: 978-1-957392-43-1
Library of Congress Control Number: 2025941884

Cover design by Amy Wheaton

Teen Queen Training

Essays after *The Seventeen Book of Etiquette and Entertaining,* 1963

Author's Note:

These essays are erasures created from *The Seventeen Book of Etiquette and Entertaining* by Enid A. Haupt, published by the David McKay Company, 1963. The edition used was the eleventh printing, April 1968.

Following standard erasure practice, no words have been added to these essays—although occasional punctuation has been—and all words/letters appear in their original order. Each chapter is contained within a single erasure essay. New words were frequently created through erasing parts of other words, but these new words were derived by selectively erasing, always retaining the letters' original order. White space between erased words/letters was eliminated to focus the reader's attention on the words and meanings I read into the found text.

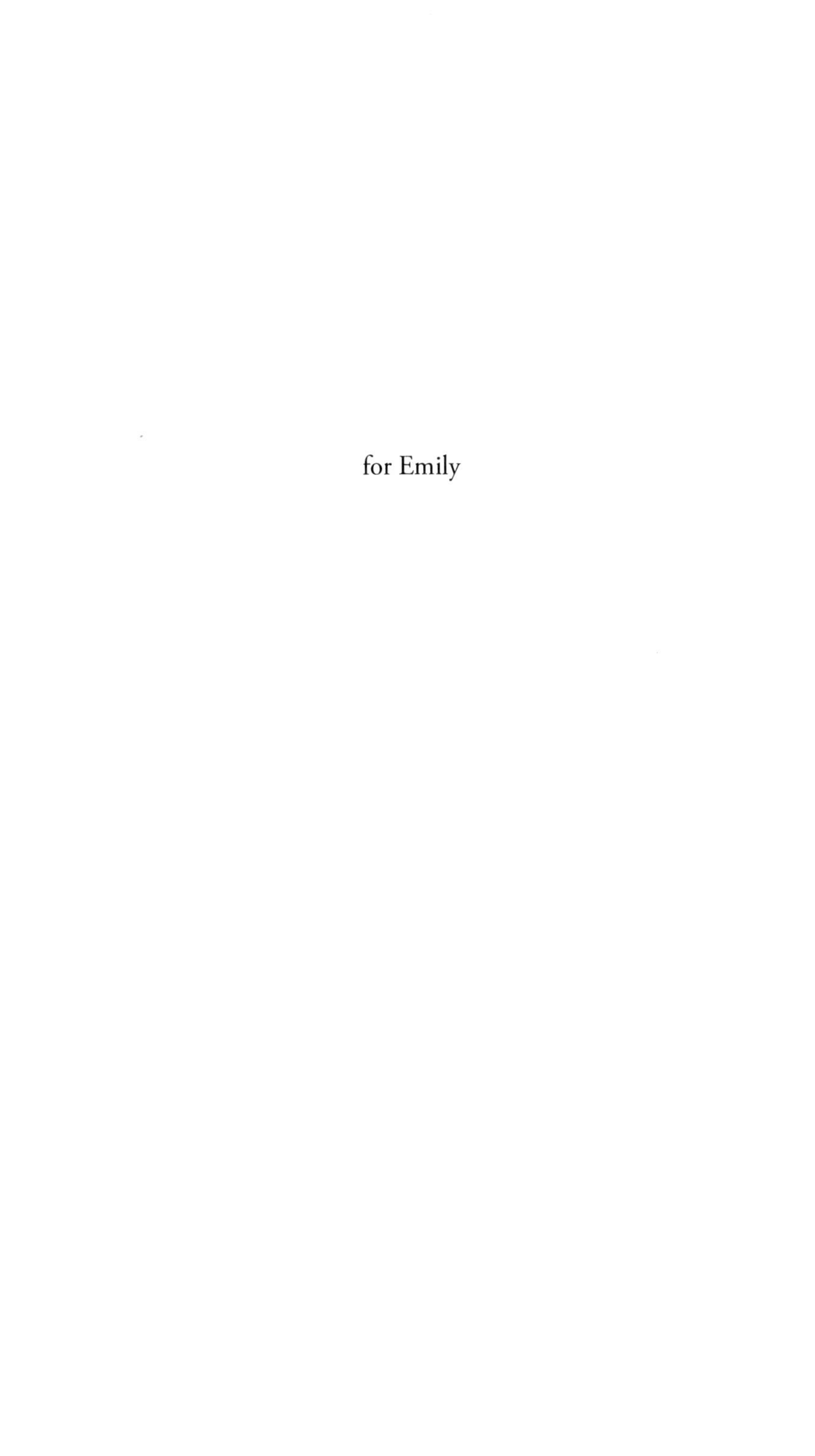

for Emily

THE seventeen
BOOK OF ETIQUETTE
AND ENTERTAINING
BY ENID A. HAUPT

teen
QUE E
NT R AINING

Table of Contents

1. Nice People: THE HABITS THEY HAVE

nice (nīs), a. Pleasing, agreeable, delightful, good, kind, considerate, or the like

Nice people have good manners. Good manners are part of a good personality. Parents and teachers emphasize manners. Columnists write about them. Thinkers think about them. Ralph Waldo Emerson, perhaps the most cheerful positive thinker of the nineteenth century, offered many little sugared maxims on manners—including these, for example:

Manners are the happy way of doing things.

Good manners are made up of petty sacrifices.

We think that good manners come from the heart, that they're the sum of the adjectives describing the word "nice" at the top of this page. *Pleasing, agreeable, delightful, good, kind, considerate.* "You couldn't ask for a nicer friend." "She's as nice as she can be." "He's the nicest boy I've ever met."

We don't think good manners blossom from a quick study of the "correct" things to do. (One could be a walking etiquette book and—like Mr. Darcy in *Pride and Prejudice*—still be far from pleasing, kind or considerate.) The rules help you to be more agreeable because they serve as guides that indicate a way of doing things with grace and good taste—guides that you respect because you want to be both pleasing and pleasant to others.

Few of us could remember *all* the rules (that's why libraries put etiquette books on the reference shelf), but each of us can have manners that are very winning. It takes some alchemy that nice people know—a brew of kindness, considerateness and common sense. And the more you use all these habits, the more they become a part of you, until you no longer have to think of them.

The kind of thoughtfulness that makes you nice to have around is all part of being

Nice on the inside Like the courteous French, who appreciate that even buying paper clips can be a pleasant experience, you try to leave the other person with a cheerful feeling after you've gone. The kind addition of a few polite words—*"Good morning . . .* May I have a box of paper clips, *please . . . Thank you"*—unquestionably makes you feel more amiable. But think also of the difference in the salesperson's day—and how your kindness can buffer the people-are-no-good effect of a rude encounter later in the day.

The point is that you're not haphazard about courtesy, reserving it to lavish

~~Nice People: The Habits They Have~~
The Habit

nice (nīs), *a.* See: *girl.*

A vacuous term in the nineteenth-century sugared maxims on the phase you want to master: teen etiquette. A pride and prejudice from a single need, to be both pleasing and pleasant to others. Remember all the rules; libraries of mistakes line the halls, noses in lockers, backs untapped. A rude or haphazard courtesy to people you want to like you (boys, girls, boys) can file you beside them, unannotated, spine cracked once.

A heap of magazines arrive monthly, the weight of the knowledge you need to absorb. You are young enough to remember the "compliment" of *how much you've grown*—all that's left is a measure of discontent at having grown too much or not enough; thin or too thin. It's not nice to make others envious. Fib, and they do a battery of tests to discover the fib. Make an honest effort to obscure the bones; pretend you have to work to achieve them. Do your part well. Believe absence is enough.

You deprive. You don't try to cadge souvenirs (snips of hair, fragments of clothing). You perform self-control in not staring at the boy you want—okay, at least you don't make eye contact. You wait for his blunt movement toward you, or away. Your job is to draw. Everyone knows the only situation is boy meets girl, boy approaches girl.

You're so hungry but you can't take the first bite. You learned the steps but still have to stand by the bleachers, swaying until you're asked.

There are things a nice person remembers not to say, because a nice person is an urn on a shelf, a vessel of others' lives. She is a Five Star notebook, her attentive records in outlined form, that no one borrows before the test. Homework that isn't collected. She holds onto it just in case.

Looks, clothes, possessions can be status traps to ask why your family doesn't belong to the club, what's the matter with your shoes, why don't you go on a diet? Nice people demur, redirect—*isn't that the last bell?*—fading into the slurry of kids dashing through the hall before the doors close.

You sit in the center row and you do not raise your hand, but you answer when you are called on. You always know the answer.

You've been inside, curling up by your bed, reading. *Are you obsessed? True crush to true love: make it happen. Ten ways to tell if it's real.* When asked about you, he said, "I mean, she's nice," and crossed his arms, that suave brutality hurting more than deliberate cruelty.

Nice is a trap, a reduction, an erasure. Nice is the eighth name on a list, everyone's friend but nobody's best, high-kicks in a cheerleader uniform, victorious boys hugging the others as you pick up their poms, sidelined for now. You know nice is aspiration and anomie; a goal and a ghoul; a girl, watching.

2. Nice To Be With: IN YOUR HOME AND NEIGHBORHOOD

If you're nice to have around, people generally want to have you around. That means you're popular, and the longing to be popular is one of the keenest desires of the human heart. There are many "secrets" of popularity, but the important one—the one that's often overlooked—is that to be truly popular means to be beloved. You can lavish money, presents, rewards of all kinds on others and still not be beloved (leaving you with a very hungry heart). You can go along with the crowd for good or for evil, for better or for worse. You can be the girl who has everything material but who has nothing.

How to be beloved? It's a personal matter between you and other people. It means always being nice, thinking of nice things to say and smothering the desire for the final word or the cruel jibe that may seem brilliantly fitting. It means being nice for your family to live with, nice for your roommate and, eventually, the person you marry to live with. It means being nice for other people to be with, in and out of school, doing paid or volunteer work, at church, at play.

Perhaps you know the quip that advises, "If you don't have enough manners to go around, save the few you have for those at home." Sad and true, for home—the place we learn manners—is where they are forgotten the quickest. It isn't just remembering to say please and thank you. There are basic qualities that make you

NICE TO LIVE WITH

you respect privacy You have a vigorous opinion about your own right to privacy—and you're entitled to it; you also make a kind and deliberate effort not to interfere with your family's privacy. Your mother's, father's, brothers' and sisters' mail is theirs and only theirs—as are their diaries, appointment books, checkbooks, bankbooks, piggy banks! Their telephone calls are not always casual, and you tactfully disappear if you realize the conversation is really not meant for you to hear. You try, try, try to convince your younger brother that listening in on the extension phone is vexing, snooping, practically dishonest—even though he thinks it's a vastly clever trick.

You knock on any closed door in your house before entering. Actually you knock on a closed door anywhere.

You ask before you borrow things large and small—your mother's stockings, the family car, your sister's pen, your brother's baseball jacket.

You keep family secrets secret: the major ones, of course, like your father's business being in a shaky state—that's obvious and instinctive—but the gossipy ones too, the kind that would really make awfully good stories, such as your mother's adding the $159 to her checking account instead of subtracting

~~Nice to Be With: In Your Home and Neighborhood~~

Not Your Hand

You can't have your keenest desire, to prove to your mother that you can be the girl who is beloved. She was. Instead: the cruel jibe, the brilliantly fitting insult, the arsenal you equip to insist you never wanted to become her. In case. And then you listen in on the extension, hoping to learn how. You borrow your mother's stock, your sister's, your brother's. You keep secrets like your father, instinctively smearing an error, ashamed.

The ones you love are as out of bounds as friends when it comes to trust—too many side-longed avoidances at the wrong hour. You hole up and sob quietly at how your crush threw spit instead of his heart (*haha* keeps playing over and over and over). You don't use your mother as a mirror; your clothes disgust her, the pit-stains remain hardened. She finds you sullen, the incense and blacklight confirmation of drugs, but you need all the help you can get to alter the way you are seen.

The money isn't a placebo; you've known enough budgetary emergencies to assume her J. Crew offer must be funded with an unrancorous reallotment of resources. They are willing to let you date now, she reminds you. She says *there's always silver that needs polishing,* but you want to be loved for the tarnish.

The balance of your failure weighs against you. To abide by her authority is to be subject to some kind of over-directed, outdated vision, but your obedience shapes you. Uncertain, *yes, Mother,* you let her purchase three-inch shorts, thighs plaguing the girls when you obviously wanted to bother a boy. Monopolizing attention damages the consoling arms of retreat, conversation truncating as you reenter.

"Can't fix envy, Mom," too wrecked to allege it her mistake. A token smile as she nods, putting the burden on the person you're not, the future you've promised.

3. Nice To Be With: AT SCHOOL AND COLLEGE

In the bigger world outside your family, there are rules that make you nice to be with:

At school You are respectful and considerate to your teachers, whether they are male or female . . .

- you say "Yes, Miss Smathers" or "Yes, Mr. Darrell," rather than "yes" or "uh-huh"
- you're silent when the bell rings for class to start
- you do your homework on time, ask for extensions only when necessary (bad habit to get into, anyway)
- you do your homework neatly—in pen or typed, except, perhaps, math and lab reports
- you pay attention in class: while the subject may be massively boring to you—or you read the book under discussion as a small child—you at least look bright and interested. (Teaching is a give-and-take operation, and an alert class makes a teacher more interesting.)
- you understand *thoroughly* that note-passing, letter-writing, doodling and whispering to friends are unacceptable classroom activities
- when you are desperately bored—and it happens to us all occasionally—you maintain your manners and air of interest by taking notes to stay awake. You can always take them in French—or list clichés or idiosyncrasies of speech. Or you can work on a tangent—observing the way the teacher presents the subject, trying to work out the outline she must have used. Or even look out for mannerisms—hers or those of members of the class—making notes for "business" in the school play or that short story you've been meaning to write
- you take part in class discussions but try never to interrupt a classmate
- you wait your turn to speak and remember to be brief so someone else will have a turn
- you take pity on the class show-off, realizing that most show-offs parade their learning because they want attention and know few ways to get it
- when a teacher explains a point to you, in class or out, you thank her
- when you're quite at sea about a point the rest of the class already understands, you wait till after class for an explanation—rather than hold up everyone while you have your problem solved in detail
- you treat all school property as if it were your own (and your father, the taxpayer, probably feels it is!). Books, lab equipment, the gym, the washroom, the furnishings, the walls and the grass—all are yours to respect and care for

~~Nice to Be With: At School and College~~

Cool

Before, you were a lightning rod. Excitement slivered through note-passing and whispering in a classroom, and you knew the cliché idiosyncrasies of positioned fear. They would court you. You knew to take pity on the class show-off; she was your best publicity, theatrical declarations that she may be quick, but no one's as fast as YOU.

Re-orientation in the east—a telescoped process of getting acquainted with new people, a new situation—however, was an unplanned plunge. New and eager to settle into routine judgments, you make friends only with girls who shut out girls who are different, confiding the story of your life to a girl you didn't know would cling to you; you didn't quickly identify it as tryout.

Bewildered newcomers just haven't learned to be realistic: grab the first outstretched hand, and use the very feminine art of appearing to be amiably confused at the situation if her unsophisticated ardor grows. It's a situation you can't live with. No one ascends with sweaty claws. The dominant cull power incrementally, chrism solemnly daubed after each invitation. You wait to pique interest, a substitute for introduction.

Every school has a locus; if you show adaptability to the customs, your season will be respected. Later, when you've settled in, center girl surrounded by acolytes once more, you can be generous, noticing shy sideliners, beckoning them to your remove. This is a gracious and efficient way to demonstrate power.

When you show the manners of a lady, boys transform into boyfriends. Braced, cultivating a haughty demeanor, you're not rushing matters. The thing is to conserve caring, quietly leaning against a post, behavior gleaned from television teens—now outdated, but you don't see the tactical shift for months.

It's the quirky ones, the girls disturbing the calm, the night owls hooting—you always regarded the belles as born into natural popularity. Boys like them just as they are. Your small, homogeneous survey held sacred that truth, and craving attraction was a certain sign of the neediness no girl should express. This unpleasant enlightenment, watching noise and pressure on a bare arm succeed, is insulting; you simply don't understand how a pedestal doesn't allure.

Frantic to appear blasé, you withdraw further, Mysteriosa in her lair, averting eye contact after making it. Doesn't anyone want a challenge? Clouds darken, tornado-swirl, electrical strikes illuminating your scarred arms, but no one remains above ground.

4. Nice To Be With: IN PUBLIC

You make or break a reputation for yourself, your school, your age group generally by the way you act in public. You can create an image of teens that is wonderful or awful, because adults react emotionally to disturbing public behavior. They reason in this summary if illogical fashion:

This girl is noisy, rude, thoughtless.
This is a *teen-ager*.
All teen-agers are noisy, rude, thoughtless.

The key word in that corollary is probably *thoughtless*. If you thought about it, would you

- *take over* a crowded street by walking three or four abreast, like an advancing army platoon?
- *buck* the oncoming traffic by proceeding up the left side of the walk when you belong on the right?
- *barge* across the street against the traffic signals, causing considerable ravage to both cars and drivers as they screech and swerve to avoid you?
- *start* a conversation with strangers or be tricked into one—when it's so simple to move quietly away (or buy a paper to read or make a phone call)?
- *plant* yourself solidly in the front of the bus instead of making way for newcomers by moving to the back?
- *cut* a bruising path through any crowd (books, bags and all) without saying "Excuse me, excuse me" all the way?
- *smoke*, chew gum, or eat on the street?
- *remain* seated on a subway, train, bus or in a waiting room while any of the following stand—an older woman, a very old man, anyone holding a young child, any handicapped or overburdened person?
- *accept* a seat from someone else without a smile and a thank-you?
- *forget* to hold a door open till the person behind you can catch it?
- *rush* through a door ahead of an older person?
- *neglect* to say "You're welcome," when thanked for holding the door or whatever?
- *block* a doorway, any entrance or exit—especially when you're in a group?
- *get out of line* on any line—from the school cafeteria to the local movie—by crowding in out of turn or trying to make the line move faster by nudging the person ahead of you?
- *blast* the car horn insistently when you're snarled in a tie-up that blasting obviously won't resolve?

~~Nice to Be With: In Public~~
Now, In Public

You make or break yourself by your teens. That's a fact. Emotional behavior, illogical fashion, nosy thoughtlessness—the key corollary is "less." You thought about it.

You advance up the left side when you belong on the right, barge against signals as others swerve to avoid a conversation. Plant yourself solidly in front, a newcomer bruising, a crow saying *Excuse me, excuse me.* You wait, holding your burden on one hip, the dread of neglect a weight, ballast. You blast a horn insistently, snarled in a tie-up that won't resolve, the noise a notice-me-anyway. Nuisance-child, you linger too long, a faint hubbub the debris you leave, a trace of trash to indicate you were there.

Your commotion took nerve, shattering silence, your blurred bedlam moderated by mollifying behaviors to be more tolerable. You simper, praising in desperate politesse the parties you pretend you had to miss. Your concern for other people's comfort is flawed; your voice retains its sweetness, your manners patient, but the ribs protrude through your empathy. A frayed operation, smiling without showing your sugar-rotted molars, without calling out the cost as you grit and pay the bill.

Like the photograph you hid [your fault; your fault or the operator's], a Sixties fake trance, peace fingers and your peeled-back flannel blown open, exposing the cheap one-sided print conspicuously on sale for only five bucks at Roses. A careless accident confessing the financial chasm, your bridge-building inept, the gossip improved by your indignant denial—there's proof.

You borrowed something fragile, expensive, irreplaceable; if you show the slightest hesitation, the loan shatters. Laugh off the damage—synchronic hurt—until you can bolster your standing. Trying to gain access is like any new enterprise: it demands new clothes.

A chance to repurpose poverty-stare, you elect a symbol of popularity—Goodwill—your white skin a kind of prepaid protection, no cost to your "slumming." An indulgent grab-bag stuffed with big names, luxury labels of yore, accepted with a sort of awe. No one else has Ralph Lauren cords. No one else has vintage DARE t-shirts. Heads turn to follow, considering the old light gleaming off your shoulders, acumen precious as gold.

You drop your voice. A restrained silence allures, full-length mink muffling the decibels of last fall, its origins forgotten until May, the yearbook preserving your pressed-lip smile, brown hair tucked behind one ear, dead eyes, the telltale flannel flipped open, bleed-through bright as the moon, a public record.

5. Boys, Boys, Boys

Any girl can get a date, have a boy in love with her, become engaged and get married. Fix these facts in your mind *and believe in them* and you will be successful at getting along with boys. Everything is in your favor because most boys like most girls—whether the girls are smashing beauties, super-smart students, energetic leaders; whether they have brilliant talents, social position or parents who invented money. (If a real, pleasant girl has one or more of those plus values—fine.) This is your answer to "I wonder what he sees in *her*." What he sees in her is plain enough (and she may be very, very plain too): he sees a girl who's thoroughly confident about being a girl—a girl who likes people, who expects them to like her, who is fun to be with. But—first she has to meet the boy.

MEETING THEM

What is the approach; how does a girl meet boys, talk to them, get a date?

There are boys around; you see them, you don't know them and you haven't figured out a way to meet them. Why can't you just say hello? In some cases, you can: you can smile and say hello to a boy who lives in your neighborhood, to a boy who goes to your school or your church. You can speak to a boy who is a member of a club you or your family belong to. Just a quick hello, not a conversation—that's too much for a start, but if you keep recognizing he's alive, the opportunity to talk will soon come. The old rule was never speak to a stranger; the modern rule is you may say hello to strange boys in known places and to known boys in strange places (you're out with friends or with your father at his club, his college, his business). Of course, you may smile and speak to anyone there. But never speak to strangers in strange places.

There isn't a boy in sight; or, nearer the truth, maybe you haven't made yourself visible. Wishing to meet boys won't make it so.

Go places To parties, even if you don't have a date. Most young parties include unattached boys and girls. If it turns out to be a couple party, help your hostess organize the games, get the food ready, do the dishes (she may have a brother or cousin, or one of the male guests who doesn't have a permanent girl may notice and think what a good sport you are). Visit three or four friends every week, even if only to lend a record or borrow a book. Making friends of girls is one of the easiest ways to meet boys. Most girls enjoy bringing people together on the least excuse.

~~Boys, Boys, Boys~~

Boys, Boss

Any girl can fix these facts.

Believe them, most boys like smashing beauties—they have social position. What he sees is a plain girl who expects to meet The Boy. There are boys around. You see them. You don't figure out a way to meet them. Why can't you just say a quick hello, not a "conversation" (that's too much for a start)? Opportunity comes in strange places—you speak to *anyone* in strange places.

There isn't a boy in sight (you made yourself visible). Wishing to meet boys won't make it so. Help a boy notice you, even if "making friends" is the excuse. Go to every event. Go if a boy might be interested. Games interest men: parades, exhibitions, shows. Watch mothers; commandeer their sons. Keep the line moving. Join a group, any group, an all-girl group (girls have brothers, girls know boys). Do something, learn a lesson, find victims. Develop a hobby; when you're good at the hobby, offer for free. Learn rapidly; boys need theses. Arrange to run into boys, find a store where men shop, things like that.

(Remember, the object is to make some boy attentive and interested. You want to be noticed, criticized. The way he looked at others.)

A boy, at last, says hi. End of conversation. You act "naturally" and "casually": there's a vacant spot next to him (you'd sit near his feet). You're devastated by what would happen if he said no.

You're waiting. He's seen you. You're so excited you're sick.

You have more time. You swear you saw him get interested. You hanker after any boy who looks moderately human: the fellow with the crag-like face, the battered boy with the crooked teeth. You never know. What about the first smile you elicit? You appreciate his liking you enough to answer your (unnerving, obvious, sincere, unsure) "No-one's-ever-said-I-was-pretty-before, I-know-you-don't-really-mean-it."

What "wolf" whistles? A whistle is a compliment. You're a girl. Yes, you like the boy. Yes, it flatters you. Yes! You can make the boy interested! The moment he's interested, you really like him! It's one of those binding situations where you have to take your chances, stalling and hoping you can honestly say you want him. You promised; you're not sure; you're wrong.

You have a raging fever. You run into the hurt all evening, ruffled by the thought that *you*'ve been inconsistent. You have to cover your traces—you're sorry, a lame half-truth. You ask him just to come to your house. He forgets. On Saturday night, you take your chances and look ethereal in white tulle. If you're wrong, you can recognize and—oops—it's dress-up! You ask him to the dance; he may or may not arrange to go with another, who's better. Let him, whatever the story is. Everyone knows. Even you.

Don't be discouraged. *Someone* says yes—arranged by friends, that known roulette, an end to the end. You want to go out and be seen: the date might produce The Man. Success is up to you. The boy will be average, but enough. You seek his advice, you keep him talking. You *really* want his opinion. "You're the one who could really tell me what to do!" (*There must be a way I can get him.*)

He may be fairly sick of enthusiasm; his attraction was being swooned over (and it sickens you). Look on him as a research project in depth: find out what girls in school he thinks are attractive, ask what he likes about their looks. Discuss whether men are more attracted by girls. You know what you think.

On the first date, you gather a lot of male point-of-view. You understand you can forget about any subject you're a brain about. He's probably a lonely soul—laugh a little less enthusiastically. Stop that mad pace—too eager. He can't stand girls who try to be better than men, smart girls who don't know how to act semi-dumb, girls who boss all the arrangements, girls who won't consider another point of view.

He never cracks your impression of a boy whose suit jackets are always too short in the sleeve. Does he do something special? Has he broken very little?

Suddenly little questions pop into your mind. If you act

young and nice, he'll like you. Right? You are fortified with an obligation he'll think is queer—you have a problem that isn't generally known—*you dislike all men.*

It's eccentric and embarrassing—you prefer your friends. Explain your story simply: "I'm too conventional, too young and untried." He can manage to get along with the problem. Oddly, he may like you for the tension, finding a bond between strength and the girl's dependence on his strength. You have to be ready; you're the slow one here. Your mother trills, *You look extra pretty when you blush!* You fill in the dead spots his mother used to handle—waiting, but not too eager. Don't make him self-conscious, don't find out that his plans include a new girl. It counts when the boy just wants to spend the evening. It's very flattering. He likes you!

Maybe. He never takes you anywhere. You maneuver. You may drive him away if you let outsiders in, if you arrange for a friend to pick you up—he doesn't give any sign of planning to take you out. You can't really ask him outright, though, because you'd be embarrassed. The trouble is that boys just don't talk. Maybe you're very hard on his needs—boys usually don't mind if you're brief and matter-of-fact. If you really like him, people think you're married, silent, a scared rabbit, icy.

Is it overdoing it to say something? He's mad when all you want to do is neck. Certain mannerisms annoy boys (he'd rather see your face in repose than busy as a bunny's). You're making him nervous. He chose you (you almost always glow). Maybe you're just being polite. You agree: below-the-belt, "still friends" when the discussion ends. Is it proper, how happy you are to be with him? Just don't announce the cheap thing unless he suggests it. Who suggests it? He does. Sound regretful.

Suppose a boy deliberately doesn't compliment you. Ruefully accept another date, sigh, one more chance. It's a pretty gesture if you hesitate a little; a boy expects you probably want to be kissed. Kiss on a first date quickly—you know he knows it.

Why doesn't he call? you wail. How can you get him back? Welcome to the group: you did wrong. When he gets around to calling you, you'll understand that it's no use—he can't explain saving time.

He used to date before he met you (back to *her* again). Maybe it will only be temporary. He enjoys keeping you guessing—he doesn't want you, so he'll probably call you. He loves his independence, etc. He liked you a lot but you really weren't his "type."

You lean to the art of being kissable, of having caught the boy. You like going out with him, you want to stay friends, you're in love. The idea of kissing becomes increasingly important, and you feel worse. Should you pretend a little? Boys kiss attractive women; quite probably that boy you're in love with is not pining for you.

A kiss is a sort of status symbol to you. What will hurt is

to pretend you don't feel wild about the boy, to get involved in the routine of a Couple in Love—the long phone calls, the letters, the necking. You keep the friends he wants to see *and* the romantic situations, evenings in a fire-lit room with a thousand love songs. On the record, you're not putting him through the oh-so-in-love paces. He has a lot of things to take more seriously. He'll find another girl. And still like you. And still like you.

You find you really like the words. You daydream about a hundred perfect ways (none of them work out). Don't worry—he knows. When he phones with his triumphs and woes, he likes the way you build him up. If hearing the words becomes important, he'll say indignantly, *Of course I love you* (which isn't the way you planned it at all).

You want him to kiss you. For weeks, he hasn't tried to snatch one little kiss. You want him to kiss you. You would like to be kissed. You have to be an aggressive snuggler—available. In case. You rest your head on his shoulder when you dance, you slip your hand in his at the movies, you linger at your doorway when he takes you home. What kind of boy is he?

He's uneasy. His mother was the glamour girl until his father made her scrub her face (very disheartening to a girl who's longed for the day she can be chic, perfect, beautiful—and look scrubbed, brushed, simple. Women make an art of doing exactly this). Then you break the spell, just as he said. *I find it hard to whisper sweet nothings to a creature,* a girl remembered as some problem he's facing.

You start an argument this time. Don't stab. Don't choke. You want to scream at his face? You should. Other people rather enjoy seeing the radiance get a little grimy. Limit it to half an hour when family and friends are milling around. A strong arm around your shoulder becomes a public matter; he needs both hands to get where you're going.

See, a boy you date steadily is acceptable around parents. They don't object. Everyone needs someone to hurt. Let your heart break quietly so he won't notice it, so he will be able to enjoy his only senior year. Or you just make it harder, trapped by your narrowness, gaslit, steadily discouraged by everyone's opinions.

Young people get the monumental strain—one person, no prospect of marriage. You lose, you stay green as May, no chance to develop security, afraid he'll put the emphasis on "friends" instead of a date (the problem). The girl with the steady beau and the girl who plays are just different. Suppose the boy's away all summer. Or suppose *you* go away; he doesn't want you to go out with anyone else. You don't, because someone would be sure to tell him, but you know this isn't very secure.

He doesn't have much time for you (but you can see him eleven pews away). You stay home. Lonely, isn't it? You could develop some outside interests of your own. There's a bittersweet happiness in the thought of that special, tender last promise. That space you cleared is now filled with clips on a sure road to spinsterhood. There's really only one way to break the system: a brisk beginning.

Boys are eager to come. Sometimes a girl is completely entranced. That's probably the best reason for the cost of loving (fairly steep for a girl). A thoughtful girl will try to every week (you don't always have to have flowers either; everyone knows). You provide exhibits, rehearsals. On a nice afternoon you suggest some outdoor spot. You explore long walks, where all kinds of entertainment abound.

Remember that there's no way you can do it without hurting. Be as kind as you can; it's a courtesy you owe him. The phone is a shabby way to escape an obligation, and the only time it's forgivable is when the boy's away. It's his decision and you'll have to go along with it. On the other hand, if you honestly can't anymore, don't say anything and be pleasant; say you're sorry but you're busy. Over and over and over. The one thing you don't tell him is the truth: you wanted it.

An ex gave you a symbol of going steady: fraternity manners, the kindest silence. His desirability's back into circulation? The word will get around fast enough. Boys are scarce (one touchy little problem); you understandably resent the idea. Be enough of a realist to know that you get the boy, you lose the friend.

He asks for his "freedom"? Make the parting tolerable—no pleading, groveling, threats that will make you ashamed. Every girl has this situation; what counts is how you learn to recognize when a boy's interest is waning and to make the break yourself. He's interested in another girl?

Make the break. You're out of tune with what attracted you in the first place. You were sincerely interested in his stories. You just…stopped, noticing no other girl is as interested in him as you were, long ago.

6. The Art Of Saying No Nicely

By now you know how to say no to a romance you no longer care to continue. But there are many other situations involving boys and girls as well, in which you'll want to say no. Even adults find it hard much of the time to locate the perfect phrase, create the right climate, in which to express their preferences without making enemies or seeming to be harsh or unpleasant.

But saying no nicely is as vital a part of your personality as doing the things that you are *sure* please people. When you express choices, you are giving others directional signals that help them to know The Real You, the person inside. What you value, what you dislike, what you want in your life and want to cast out of it—all are important things for your friends, or friends-to-be, to know.

So don't hesitate to say no; people will respect you for it, if you learn to say it honestly and nicely. And here are guides to some of the ways.

how to say no nicely The way you say it varies with what you're being asked, who's asking it and how. Most of the time you can say no lightly and change the subject. Then again there are times when directness is the kinder approach: like pulling off adhesive tape, it hurts less when you do it decisively.

There are many things you may want to refuse at one point or another in your life. Relatively easy things, such as a dance or a date. "Statusy" things, such as a drink, a cigarette, going some place you know is off limits. Entangling things, such as a loan or a favor—or going steady. Things that grate your conscience, such as being asked to do a friend's homework. Emotionally loaded things, such as petting or necking. Or just a kiss. Probably the most we can do is to give some examples, which you can adapt to your life. (There may be just one way to eat an artichoke, but there are a thousand ways to say no.)

how to refuse a date so he'll ask again You say you're sorry, you have a date, you're going out with the family, or whatever. *And you add,* "I wish I could—I would have loved it, Jack"—something that tells him you're not handing out a routine no.

when you want to turn him down Say, "I'm sorry; I just can't" without explanation (even if he asks for one). Thank him for asking you but don't lead him on so he'll ask again. To be too kind when you mean NO is to be cruel.

how to refuse a dance Say you promised the dance to someone else, you're waiting for your date, you can't Charleston, you'd love to have some punch. Just remember you can't refuse to dance with one boy and rush to the floor

~~The Art of Saying No Nicely~~

Say No Nice

You say no to romance; you no longer care. Boys seem harsh, directional signals you want to cast out. Don't people respect you? You learn to guide the way you say it, you change the subject. The kinder approach, like pulling off adhesive tape, hurts.

You refuse easy things, "statusy" things. You favor things that grate. You ask to do loaded things: petting or necking. Or just a kiss. You adapt; there are a thousand ways. You say you're going, whatever, it's all a routine. You mean to be cruel, to refuse, you're waiting, you can't—then rush to the floor without explanation. A boy deserves a welcome, and you need to matter. LOVE? Not just now, thanks. You don't have to say why. It gets pretty dreary.

You've just enough self-respect to fend off personal questions, they seem never to refuse. To go steady is like proposing—too severe. A kiss under the mistletoe is a scene over nothing. If a boy has plans, you start the feminine defense of laughing. It's very hard to kiss a laughing girl. You get a glass of water, *are you asking me to MARRY you? You're acting like an octopus.*

The real problem for every unattached female is the expectation that a kiss has value. It seems silly to refuse to kiss him when you know you'll kiss him, when you know all you'll spare yourself: the humiliating feeling of half-interest. You wriggle seductively, you push yourself, a lot more like Maybe or Please, fair game. Blank or bored, you look like a fast girl—too pointed, too tight, too short—the obvious need, the over-use.

You lean against the boy's car—a party with lights dimmed, a make-out session, expecting his manly reputation to be proven; less all the time. So you will go solo to a boy's room, avoid situations in which the "no" problem will come up.

7. Good Sports Go Places

GOOD SPORT It's the classic description of someone who's nice to have around—the good companion; the good opponent; the good-natured, easy, noncomplaining guest. Without sportsmanship the game's a bore. A good sport—girl or boy—is meticulous about obeying the rules. In general they are these:

- play your best; no matter how far behind you are, keep trying
- be a generous opponent—slow to take advantage of a technicality for yourself, quick to give another the benefit of the doubt
- take defeat gracefully: praise the victor's game instead of excusing your own (never *"I've been sick!"*)
- accept victory modestly; find something valid to say about your opponent's game—an unreturnable backhand, not one three-putt green
- never display "righteous" impatience about the game's being delayed, someone's talking during the play; no glares, sharp words, requests to play the point over
- accept criticism for breaking a rule with a quick apology
- call any infringement of the rules on yourself—particularly one not noticed by your opponent
- never criticize your partner
- adapt easily—and without complaint—to the house rules of the game when you are a guest

The rules sum up the good sport who's always asked to play, to sail, to join in whatever plans are being made.

Some sports have very specialized rules and customs—some for safety, some for protecting the golf course or the ski slope, some to add to the challenge of the game, some to give the participants every chance to play at the top of their abilities.

If you have fallen in love with a particular sport, look for magazines and books devoted to the sport; libraries and clubs usually have them. You'll enjoy the discussions of all the refinements of the game and ways to improve your playing. General rules for a few of the major sports follow here:

BOWLING

- be punctual: lanes are crowded these days, and you owe it to teammates and opponents to be on time, ready to start
- be ready to bowl when it's your turn—and *not* off buying peanuts or chatting
- when another bowler takes his stance, be attentive and quiet; say nothing, do nothing that will distract him

~~Good Sports Go Places~~

Good Sorts

It's the classic description of someone who's nice, good, noncomplaining: a bore.

You keep trying to take advantage of a technicality—you doubt your own modesty (something valid, unreturnable, righteous, delayed). Sharp words, a quick apology—infringement you notice, adapt easily, without complaint. You are a good sport who's asked to play, to join. Plans are being made. Rules and customs protect the challenge—some participants, at the top of their abilities, fall in love. With magazines and books devoted to all the ways to improve, you follow, ready to start when it's your turn, attentive. Nothing will distract his approach.

You never, never take your time. You slip, you distract, stand to the side. You cast a shadow that might distort his cue, go back when you're connected, bend over the table.

Cardinal rule: test before diving into dangerous horseplay beyond your depth. Anyone can get caught in an undertow. Running is universally frowned on; one bone can ruin the rest. To keep him, you tie him up.

You want to ask if that's his practice too. You hold up while you scuffle through the pachysandra, doubtful; you think you've won. You flub a crucial point, say distinctly, "I'm awfully sorry," moan on and on about it. You are practicing, you crowd in on someone else, idling; it's maddening to see waste. You see others waiting.

Surrender? Needless to say, beginners find that both hard and scary, close to a hazard, gouging ruts in ice. You fall, you land in a lump, watch the boys abbreviate a ban. They move on to expert terrain, ready and able. You can't control a collision: losing one's heart is obvious as a cliché. You smooth over your vocabulary; your binding has opened, you have gotten tangled in the spill. You repair the damage. You're a prime target.

You gather enough force and momentum to shatter, as dangerous as a hurled spear. Careless, you're that careless, you yell, you break, you did not expect you would not be asked again. Sex is the absolute boss and is not to be argued with. There's no extra room. Crush out a cigarette—he is unrelenting on the subject—sit down when you're told to, and on the side you're told to. Don't grab or do anything without orders. Always wear rubbers.

You boomerang backward; hard to maintain that approach. He does not care; someone else is rattling into his line of vision. This is not fair. You veer in the direction of another person as a warning; he releases. You smooth out the scuff you made, the sign of a couldn't-care-less attitude, but you're lost. You jam up the progress. You call it on yourself, your temper, yourself. You try to be depressed, but you invite faster play. The tension you create smothers resentment, makes his game worse. Your game is at its brilliant best.

You open a gate, latch it securely behind you, remember all those movies. You skim by inexperience, bolt, nerves-on-edge, protected from unnecessary poking. You walk in front of a beautiful beast, offer sugar, your hand flat as a plate. He can mumble it up with his lips; you will retain all your fingers.

You light a match, break it in two, drown it and stamp the remains. You leave in good order; you're certain everyone knows. You make sure branches and twigs you've pushed back snap in the face of whoever's directly in back of you. You remember that. You leave your property and it's all right; you pay cash, you smile and thank-you.

Ready. Shine your shoes. Hang up your dress.

You leave the room in apple-pie order—towels in the hamper, tissues in the wastebasket, no clothes allowed. You are responsible, you go to your parents, ask what rules are frowned on, rules you'll want to learn to keep interruptions at a minimum. You can be competent and content. You have a long sundown: you get wrinkled, baggy, prepared with pocket overshoes, a waterproof covering for your hair. Girls are handsomely dressed; a plain little dress will define you. You respect that what is impeccable may be impossible.

And the funny thing is that you act bewildered when you find you've chosen wrong. You have real problems: a muddy, uneven field, a rocky road, the wind, the snow, the silence.

8. When You Go To Proms And Dances

Call it a dance, a prom, a cotillion, a ball—it's still one of the greatest occasions for fun, dressing up, seeing old friends and making new ones. The music, the flowers, the gaiety all inspire an evening of carefree happiness.

What will you wear? If it's your first school prom, you may be puzzled, and your beau, equally confused, may ask you what he should wear. The dance committee may think it has everything solved by announcing that the dance is "formal." At many high-school proms, a plain dark suit with a white shirt and dark bow tie is the accepted formal dress for boys. At others, the term indicates black tie and a dinner jacket. Ask an upperclassman or a teacher to set you straight.

Remember any dance is your beau's party even if it's your school and you've invited him to go with you. Give him the tickets when he calls for you and let him make arrangements to get you to the dance. (Don't chauffeur him in your father's car.) The same code holds for suggestions about what to do after the dance. Going with the crowd to so-and-so may not be in his budget plans. Carry this as far as not agreeing to plans proposed by a couple you've double-dated with for the dance until you've talked to your date; give the boy a chance to take the lead.

About flowers Is it all right to hint for flowers? Yes, if it's for a prom where every girl will wear them *and* if you know the boy can afford it. Don't ever hint for an orchid; carnations could be as pretty with your dress. Give your date some idea of the color of your dress beforehand so he'll know what to get.

Who pins on your flowers? The boy may do it, if he can do so adroitly (this depends on him) and modestly (this depends on your dress). It's usually easier, though, for you to thank him and pin it on yourself—or ask your mother's assistance. Large safety pins, incidentally, attached invisibly from inside your dress, provide better anchorage for flowers than do corsage pins. And they're less apt to spear your date during the dance.

• *How are flowers worn?* See pages 168-169 for all you need to know about this.

~~When You Go to Proms and Dances~~
You, Prom, A Dance

A dance, a prom, a cotillion, a ball—one of the greatest puzzles.

You think it has everything solved, formal and accepted. *Your* dance, *your* beau, *your* school. *You* invited him to go with you. *You* make arrangements, chauffeur him in *your* car, suggest what to do after the dance—not his plans; plans proposed by *you*.

You give the boy a chance to take the lead. Is it all right to hint? If it's for a prom? You know the boy could get you flowers. It's easier, though, to pin it on yourself—safe, attached invisibly, anchorage—less apt to spear your need. You allow plenty of time to get the mechanics of fixing your hair, your dress is perfect (you think; you planned). You're unspottable.

Your date says no compliments.

You're a mythical princess! A real, live movie queen who owned a chunk of the world! Your date should return the favor. He's a stranger to most of your friends. You long for a heart-to-heart—you've been temporary (he is from out of town). You are vanishing fast.

Most women keep out of the corners and stalk other

quarry. The two of you have been with each other so long you feel a claustrophobia, but you don't want to refuse just now—the custom has its advantages. One obvious problem: a boy may abandon a girl. You sit this one out; you escape to the ladies' room for repairs, a wallflowers' refuge, a group of girls few have the courage to penetrate. You want to change partners, quietly disappear, crush duty.

(There have been vague rumblings of discontent through the evening)

The boy can't dance. He's hopeless. You walk off the floor, certain. He's clumsy. Online, you have an assigned place—*don't interfere with it,* you repeat over and over (and know it, and everyone else will know it too).

Weapons are outstretched arms. They have no idea. They're going to a parked car in the moonlight, so serious they look as if they couldn't possibly be cheek-to-cheek. You can't follow. He wants to go right home, a snake in a hole, but not you.

9. 16 Point Plan For Making Good On College And Prep School Weekends

There are two sure signs you've been a success at a school or college weekend. First, you had a marvelous time: this puts you halfway up the ladder. Second, you're asked again: you may have to wait for this, but it's the definitive mark of success.

WANT TO HAVE A GOOD TIME?

1. When you accept, ask your beau where you will stay.

   Your parents might want to get in touch with you. If you will be billeted in a club or a fraternity house, or a dorm which has been cleared for the boys' dates, you won't need to pay for your room. Other arrangements may mean you'll need extra money to pay for your room; the answer to who pays varies in different parts of the country, so if you're not sure, ask the boy (on the day you leave) if you may pay for the room.

2. Ask what festivities have been planned; ask if he'll let you know any new plans.

   You'll have a better idea of what clothes to take if you know everyone in his house is going sailing, swimming, skiing or whatever on Sunday. You won't need a dance dress if the annual college show is held Saturday or if poetry, folk songs and coffee are the weekend special.

3. Buy a round-trip ticket or arrange for a ride home before you get to the campus.

   Transportation is your problem, your expense.

4 Talk to a girl who's weekended at the school recently—not your mother, not your aunt. Times change.

   Ask her what to wear, what the climate is like, how many parties are likely. Get her opinion of what the boys are like, what places to avoid, the best method of getting there and back—bus, car, train, plane.

5. Ask the same girl what the room-visiting rules are.

   At some colleges, parties after the game are standard but there is a curfew hour at which all rooms must be clear of girls. At others, room-visiting is forbidden. A sensible habit is not to visit unless another girl or couple is with you.

6. List special things you might need before you pack; the nearest drugstore may be miles away from where you're staying.

   Anti-allergy pills, oversize curlers, toothbrush and other staples? Repair tools, such as cellophane tape, safety pins, small sewing kit, travel iron,

~~16-Point Plan for Making Good on College and Prep School Weekends~~
16 on A Weekend

You're halfway up the ladder. You wait for the definitive mark of success (a date). You may need other arrangements.

"He'll let you know"? Yet everyone is going sailing/swimming/skiing on Sunday! You want poetry, folk songs, coffee, but you'd settle.

How many parties are likely? At some, there is a room clear of girls, forbidden. A sensible habit is not to visit unless another girl is with you. You might pack repair tools, such as antiseptic cream, Band-Aids, sunglasses, a scarf, rubbers. Comfort wherever you can; parties go on forever, soggy potato chips and wilted carrot sticks the ballast.

You drink to prove you're trying it and know how. You ask for a twist of lemon peel. You want to curb the next sport who's eager to fix you a drink—some "funny boy"—but you say nothing, manage quietly. He probably has money at home, so you turn him into one of *those* bachelors who see girls as an assignment to complete. Go with him when he asks you, but if he doesn't, be glad—his silence is like his friends: impossible.

This weekend, you found the rival of your future dates: parties.

It's your move to end the evening's gaieties. But you can't turn in now, so you sit up all night listening to a guitar, necking with the lights turned low, "young love." You suggest, sweetly, that you'd love to walk around the campus with him, but he flinches. He says you seem to be a Great Girl, then leaves.

10. When You Eat Or Entertain In Restaurants

a date for dinner What a wonderful way to spend the evening with someone you like—talking, laughing, perhaps dancing or listening to music . . . and—oh, yes—eating a very good dinner as well. You'll enjoy the evening even more if you aren't gnawed by constant little worries: "Which fork is which?" "What should I order?" "How can I find the ladies' room?" "What should I do when he pays the check?"

entering a restaurant When you walk in with your beau, let him open and hold the door for you. Unless a coat rack is provided, he will check his coat and probably ask if you would like to check yours. Don't, unless it's a soaking-wet raincoat. You wear your coat to the table, throw it back off your shoulders and sit on it, as you would at the theater. (The reason for this difference between the sexes: many restaurants, fearful of what could happen to fur coats crushed in a checkroom, refuse to handle any feminine coats—right down to the most durable tweed. A second reason: you spare your date the tiny, but additional, expense of having to redeem your coat when he redeems his.) You may check bulky packages, an umbrella, overshoes and anything else which might obstruct service at your table. If you're wearing a hat, leave it on—unless it's a rain hat, of course. Gloves? Wear them to the table, then take them off as soon as you sit down, lay them on your lap or put them in your bag. Never, never, never wear gloves at a table. That's a mannerism, not manners.

If a waiter or headwaiter leads you to your table, you follow him and your date follows you. The waiter pulls out your chair and hands you, then your date, a menu. If it's a more do-it-yourself sort of restaurant, your date leads you to the table, pulls out your chair and hands you a menu. The point to remember is that a man should always precede you to the table and to the door when you leave, to cut a path through the surging crowd, so to speak. However, if your date steps aside to let *you* precede *him*, don't be indecisive. Just go on ahead.

seating As a girl you get the choicest seat at the table, the one with the best view or farthest from the door. If the restaurant is one with banquettes (long, upholstered seats) running along the wall, the waiter pulls out the table, you slide into the banquette seat and your date sits in a chair on the opposite side of the table. Or you might be seated side by side on the banquette. Whatever the case, *you* are seated first. Don't try to clamber into the seat by yourself; hesitate long enough to give the waiter, or your date, the opportunity

~~When You Eat or Entertain in Restaurants~~
You Entertain Rest

A date! An evening with someone you like! Yet…a "very good" evening? You are gnawed by constant little worries: *what should I?—how can I?—what should I do?*

Let him open you. He will check—you're soaking wet. You throw back your shoulders—*you would*—but fearful of what could happen, he may demur. You spare your date the expense of having to redeem anything which might obstruct service, lift a hem, hand on your lap, no never-never-never mannerisms.

If he leads, you follow. He pulls out your hand, a do-it-yourself sort. The point to remember is that a man should always precede; you leave a path, so to speak. Don't be indecisive. Just go on ahead.

The coquette pose is boring. You want a seat. You hesitate long enough to give your date the opportunity to help you (you are usually on the floor—it has seen some wear). Boys call, you meet after-hours downtown, or in vastly separated suburbs, a convenience. You arrive first. If you cannot see him after ten minutes, get comfy. Time may weaken you; you'll surely weaken his pride. Some men are especially complimented if you don't wait. There is always an exception (you'll find a few others later), though it's part of the ritual to ask what you like, whether you wish these choices.

It often adds up to more.

You suggest this, blithely ask him for everything from soup to sundae; he gives you less, which you take. Or refuse. No reason, no reason you can offer (you bury your head and agonize, stare off in space). You change your stance, you doubt him. You'd like to rewrite your entire order.

You appear forgotten. You tap your place with your forefinger—*hello? You are a marvelous Scandinavian!* You are bewildered and a bit dubious. You silently drop, dive under the table, retrieve your date (he should rise for any girl, for a woman the age of your mother, even).

You move on, a lady about it, something taken back (you don't ask, as you know by now). You never complain. This impresses no one. He is surly and generally impossible; you appear solicitous and attempt to right matters. You don't leave, though.

Everything's so strange—that's part of the "fun," experimenting. Attempting to manipulate him is not new to you. In utter privacy, you give yourself a searching once-over: your major reconstruction is an excuse, insufficient, embarrassing. You fix your face in the washroom, a terminal failure. It's still early—you offer your house, finish with a *what-do-we-do-now* expression. You're in the position of having to suggest; he obviously hasn't budgeted it into the evening. It's thoughtless to suggest further entertainment when you are an unreliable mistake, uncorrected, sitting nervously.

But you pull out your longing, a sort of velvet rope barring your red-headed heart alone, dividing the end from the varying cost of your honor. You obstruct. You tell him you might be open to seeing him again and linger behind, dawdling. You hover, waiting, the surest way to feel more at home.

11. You're A Spectator: ATTENDING THEATRES, MOVIES, MUSEUMS AND SPORTS EVENTS

Performers need a good audience to inspire them to do their best. This is as true of sports as it is of theater and concert-hall performances. A baseball player needs the excited support of the fans to spur him on to break the home-run record. The school team needs the cheers of the crowd to get that last touchdown and victory. An actor can make his role bigger than life-size if the audience is with him. An artist can interpret a piano concerto so it glitters with excitement. Dancers can make ballet a shimmering experience instead of just a display of technical skill. For better or for worse, you and the performers are one for a few hours.

The point of entertainment is to enjoy the performance. Manners like these will make you a good member of the audience:

A boy asks you to a movie or show you've seen, and it's one you don't want to see again. Do you go anyway? No. You'll be poor audience material, restless and bored, and distress your date. He wants the evening to be a success, so say something like "I'd love to go with you, Bob, but I really ought to tell you I've seen that one. It just isn't a show you'd go to twice." If he doesn't suggest another show or idea for the evening, you can mention a movie you'd like to see or records at your house . . . but nothing that would cost more than the show.

A boy asks you to a movie you don't care to see or one your parents don't want you to see. Do you tell him the truth? Be frank and say, "I'd rather not see that movie. How about . . .?" If he asks why you're against the movie, tell him briefly: "I don't like horror pictures any more" or "I read the review and I don't think I'd enjoy that kind of movie" or "I'm sorry; my parents asked me not to see it." Don't launch into a crusade about it, though.

Be ready when your date calls, so you'll be on time for the performance. Most men like to see the teams warm up, like the excitement that precedes a game or a show. It's a courtesy to the performers and to the other members of the audience when you arrive in time to be seated and have your coat and bag disposed of before the event begins. If you're late at the theater, wait for seating until the end of the first scene; at a musical, wait until the burst of applause following a number. At the ballet or opera, the usher won't seat you during the first number or act unless you're sitting in a box. At a concert you will not be seated until the first number is concluded.

~~You're A Spectator: Attending Theatres, Movies, Museums and Sports Events~~
A Spectator Event

The true theater of a girl glitters with excitement, a shimmering display of technical skill: the point is the performance. You've been restless and bored. You want to be a success, so you don't suggest the evening you'd like—that would cost more than the show you'd have to give. Horrid, his crusade about how *staying in is so lame*—operatic!

Your first number is concluded; to spare embarrassment, you stand at the window until he collects you. You will be good, you will be satisfactory even if he's grumpy. You prevent a scowl and grumble if you seem super fun!

You'd love to shrug off your program, but how? This unreasonable tradition that "a lady should not be unkindly" is your fate if you won't endanger that stiffening across a table, that veiling cage, the question that will disturb him. You bridle, neatly fold your opposition, shed it gracefully. Your mission: to thread your way back by making yourself as small as possible (the aisle is narrow).

You deliver a particularly good line; you're the only one who appreciates it.

You take your cue when he turns—selection is concluded—pauses like paragraph breaks, not the ends of chapters. He rises, rigid. A certain amount of foot-stamping and an outcry is expected; you finish, downbeat, quietly, sadly, forgivable. It is a performance.

You reflect upon your heart—tempting to smudge, spoil, break the exhibition. You will make the job easier. You do a little research for a preview of what is to come; you know the game. It's wise to appear unknowing so he can instruct you, to turn to him and say, *What's a sport?* to cuddle, nuzzle, wrestle—you know where the action is. He is breathing heavily past your ear, in your lap, your territory, beyond the boundaries, the wrong time, a serious moment to taunt the player.

If anyone had wanted to take it, he could have (he should). See: you, a full-blast radio, a country road, deserted, unforgivable.

12. On The Move: PLANES, TRAINS, BUSSES; MOTELS, HOTELS AND SHIPS

The best travelers are

open-minded—they love new places, new friends, new experiences

self-reliant—they know at least roughly how to get where they are going; they cope tearlessly with little travel tragedies such as late arrivals and misplaced luggage

organized—they can always find their tickets; they look neat, and so do their suitcases

considerate—they are quiet; they don't spread their belongings about on train seats which aren't theirs; they don't leave a trail of litter behind them

comfortably dressed—in wrinkle-resisting, easy-fitting clothes, in colors and patterns that don't show smudges readily. They have a sweater handy for extra warmth, a raincoat that doubles as a topcoat. They wear shoes intended to be *walked* in.

pleasing to the eye—on buses, planes and trains, they dress tastefully, conservatively. Girls forego shorts or slacks in favor of a skirt; they choose an easy, wrinkle-resistant skirt when a long ride on a plane or sit-up train is in prospect. Young travelers of both sexes are prepared for social emergencies: a boy has a tie, a girl has some form of head covering—a scarf, net bonnet, packable hat—for quick compliance with the custom of a restaurant, a concert, a church, an unexpected party.

Special advice

TRAVELING BY CAR

- Take your ordinary good driving manners along when you travel by car—and be especially careful about littering. (Travel trash seems to accumulate faster on a long trip than on a short one.) In national parks and at public camp and picnic grounds you should be really meticulous about cleaning up after yourself—and about extinguishing campfires, crushing out cigarettes and breaking up matches before throwing them away.
- With your family? If everyone is in a contented mood, the whole family will have a better time. You can help by being patient with parents when they reminisce or carry on about the history of sights you see. You can also take on some responsibilities in order to make the trip more of a vacation for them—writing the post cards to Grandma and the thank-you's to friends you visit along the way; emptying the litter bags; taking charge of the road maps, perhaps learning to read them. If younger brothers and sisters go

~~On the Move: Planes, Trains,~~
~~Busses; Motels, Hotels and Ships~~
Lanes

The others know how to get where they are going. They cope tearlessly with tragedies, they belong, they don't leave a trail of litter behind them or show smudges. They intend. They are resistant. You prepare for compliance, your manners careful and meticulous. You extinguish fires before you reminisce—emptying the road maps, perhaps learning to read them—and you take on ghosts, you guard a forest (it won't help).

You long for a hand to hold (or just a boy) to take you, complete you. An end starts as a glorious adventure, but the habit of constant exposure (a fault of which you are aware) goes off-key quickly; the length of your itinerary is the problem. You put the balance of your desire in a safe place, and in another, keep the record of all that is lost. You thought you'd made notable efforts, but you need, you need. You don't have restrictions, you have other problems: a shortage of popularity, a service curtailed to a long-distance destination. You don't exist.

You wrestle with your destiny, your station (it is with you at all times). An unhappy experience, to be left. So you try to make friends with a crashing bore, a wolf to your Little Red Riding Hood. You know. You talk to him awhile; your problems have begun.

He is tall, blond, devastating. He says he is at Yale (you think it may be true). He wonders why you're reading Eliot. You let him buy you dinner, let him in your home. You don't know his friends or family, you don't know what he is really like. You say, sweetly, "I'm really sorry, but. Umm." He persists, and you change, subtly. A different conduct. You meet again under carefully fenced circumstances, melodramatic, not where you wanted to go. You occupy the night, a necessary luxury, your latest misstep (you simply can't cope) girdling a different matter. You back into the corridor, pull a curtain across your mistake. He won't find out.

A journey long-distance, a room, a procedure less formalized. At specified points he stops, he announces, your time runs out. He is the agent of the condition. You claim that custom allows your weight, your heft (you're allowed, but you will pay). You are instructed, you obey, you adjust. You're well-equipped for that. He may give you a gracious and sincere thanks; that's expected.

You hear a tone change, an eerie whistle, a reminder: you don't count now. You find yourself in a terrible light, an emotion you swat (he has a club). You can't keep your place unless you save the seat in front of you. You don't wander off.

Boys are under no obligation to a girl. You won't get the sort of consideration you were promised. You moan and heave and stand in the rain; your slot unlocks, turns on, opens and shuts, opens and shuts. You are sure everything is in good working order. You call a boy, but he refuses to respond to your coaxing. You change, out of line. He does not appear. You meant to be used, not taken home. You cannot settle for a boy if he won't come. You stay modest, a young girl, grimly pleasant, a maid marked by your hunger.

A dream, to put yourself in the hands of a boy, hips and hotels, a guide you need, a passport to desire. He does it, it doesn't hurt, he can save you. You travel, you visit, you need proof of your attraction. You won't find the things you need (the kind of dress you'd wear to a prom, specific plans that require one).

You rack up moments, emergency items to remove the silence. One picture is worth thousands of words he doesn't say. The expense of duty may cancel out the bargain. You remember no more than you would at home—you supply information about your certainty. It is not wanted. You don't have the vaguest idea why the prospect is terrifyingly remote. You clutch yourself. You have plenty to do before that moment when he is nudging away from you. You make a stab at being more fun.

It is really quite simple. You go through customs that embarrass you. You do it neatly and completely (you save yourself time in the long run; one night is everything you'll need). You are as secure as possible. When you want something from the one you want to love you, you'll strain your rules, folding horizontally at hipline, the potential active.

You're unhooked, released, arranged, but your destiny will sneak in. You turn on full force, leave the door closed for thirty minutes, ready in another half hour. You know all about how to be open-minded.

A girl can set a poor example if what's wrong with one person characterizes everyone. She is eager to think, talk, act, react differently. She's not eager to make comparisons between life at home and life as a girlfriend (when in Rome...well, you know). She is extra careful, she pays attention to boy-girl customs. She isn't given a great deal of respect. She hasn't managed to solve her problems, but she is without rancor. A boy is a language she can poorly pronounce.

13. Car Talk: THE RULES OF THE ROAD

A good (*safe, polite*) driver knows the rules of the road, especially those which apply in his state. These are usually available, in nonlegal language, in booklets obtainable from a state's Department of Motor Vehicles. You must know them to pass the written examination for your license; you should remember them as long as you drive. While this chapter isn't concerned with how to signal for a turn or how many feet to park from a hydrant, there are a few politeness pointers which relate to the rules. Rudeness on the road *may* not be strictly illegal, but it comes close and, because it's unexpected and irritating, it's often just as dangerous.

- *Constant lane-hopping,* even if you remember to signal before switching from one lane to another, is maddening to those in front and behind and could result in a collision.
- *Bumper-hugging* is just as annoying (as well as unsafe).
- So is *failing to dim your lights* for oncoming traffic or for a car you are following closely. (You blind other drivers with the glare of your headlights.)
- *Roaring ahead* at a stop light as soon as it changes can terrify drivers with slower reactions. On the other hand, dawdling is also bad mannered.
- *Turning abruptly* after a last-minute flash of a direction signal causes following drivers to jam on their brakes—or maybe to bump into you.
- *Refusing to let a car enter your lane* when it's pulling out of a driveway into a stream of traffic is pure selfishness—hardly worth the time it might save.
- *Double-parking* must be done sometimes (while you wait for your mother to emerge from the hairdresser, for instance). Keep the motor running so you can move out of the way if necessary.
- *Thoughtless parking:* blocking access to a friend's driveway or garage. Sometimes you can't help it when there's a jam of cars at a party or a meeting—but be prepared to move your car promptly and cheerily if another driver wants to leave before you do.
- *Illegal parking:* You'll probably get a ticket if you leave your car in a no-parking zone, too close to a hydrant or in front of a crosswalk. Did you know you can also get one for thoughtlessly blocking someone's driveway?

Less-than-good car manners:

- Leaving a trail of candy wrappers, banana peels and other debris along the highway (some cities and states fine those who litter). You can easily collect your trash in a paper bag and leave it in a trash can at a gas station, a roadside rest area—even at home. Equally thoughtless: strewing litter about any picnic

~~Car Talk: The Rules of the Road~~

The Rules

Good, safe, polite: you know, you remember. You come close. It's unexpected, it's dangerous. You want a collision.

Hugging is just annoying, failing, blind. Others roar ahead, changed; slower reactions and dawdling is bad, but a last-minute flash of a directional brake (refusing to enter) is pure selfishness. Hardly worth it. Sometimes, while you wait to emerge, you block access to a friend. You can't help it when he wants to leave before you do. You probably get too close. You know you get thoughtless, leaving a trail of debris he can easily collect, but won't.

You come across as nothing less than the remnants of someone else. You inconvenience, you hang back in the rearview, a clown-car-at-the-circus so full of ends that you can hardly maneuver. It's not necessary. Boys are worse offenders than girls, deafening and hard to handle when getting too affectionate. You're more sedate, but you hear the siren call of need, a blemish.

You require constant care; they haven't the foggiest notion. You dart between cars, walk facing the traffic. You can't avoid an accident. Girls can be reckless for the sake of hands on skin. You can't stop, you demand complete attention, you climb from front seat to back seat while the car is moving. You disturb no one.

Behave. You'll remain a child, cranky and restless, played out. You're madly in love but shrewd. You never, never advise a boy on how to change. That way lies spinsterhood. This is one of those agonizing customs. You accept the obstacles of tight skirt, high heels, low-slung manners. You wait. You fill the endless interval by pretending to rummage about—you stare, and then you hop out by yourself; return, wait a second to see if he wants you. You want to make him feel like Jack the Ripper.

You'd rather be a grownup. An older person. A woman your mother's age. You reach for a maturity you haven't shown. You do your arithmetic before he starts the division. You can't be stopped. You can't be discreet.

He belongs to you and you are covetous about your need, inconsiderate in your requests. You make sacrifices for the sake of harmony. You are understanding and accommodating, you're consistently thoughtful, you lick out the ash trays, sweep out the sand.

You're underage, you're awkward, you're a teen and you don't want to be. You want the house, the college parties, the roses in the cheeks, a boy you like offering a future, the dizzy heights of ownership, a status symbol. Covert, constant repair will become your condition. You doubt, you test, you risk, you never learn. No one will instruct a girl who wants to learn about a trap.

14. When You Speak

The way you talk gives listeners a word picture of you that's as revealing as a candid camera. It tells whether you're sensitive, cultured, kind, cheerful. It describes your family, your friends, your schooling and your interests. Your manner of speech is one of the most important parts of your personality, as basic as the color of your eyes—yet a part of you easily improved.

Do you know how you sound? A simple method of finding out is to cut a record of your voice at a fair, an amusement park or a recording studio—or to make a tape recording if you know someone with a machine. The two things that surprise many people the most are the pitch—much higher than you expect—and the marked regional accent. (Like the darling Southern girl we know who said, "Now how'd he guess Ah'm fum the South?") The high pitch is something to correct, because nearly everyone would sound more attractive with more bass and less treble—particularly girls whose voices can quickly spin from soprano into a squeak, a shriek or a whine. The marked regional accent is another matter. It's a very nice facet of your personality to be able to convey by the sound of your voice the information that your family comes from Savannah or Boston or Dallas: it makes you somebody right away. If you want a standard to rate your speech against, make it this: do you sound like the nicest people in your home town?

Lack of exercise is a prime reason for a voice's sounding less than perfect. Singers, as well as actors, have fine speaking voices, because daily vocal exercises keep their jaws from becoming stiff, their tongues sleepy and their lips lazy. Singing a little every day will help keep your vocal apparatus in better condition. (Sing in the shower, if your family is unappreciative.) Another excellent exercise is to read or talk aloud in front of a mirror: you watch, you listen, and your speech improves magically in a few weeks. Here are five sentences you might read aloud slowly, giving every sound its proper value:

1. For distinct enunciation, every word, every syllable, every sound must be given its proper form and value.
2. Think of the mouth chamber as a mold in which the correct form must be given to every sound.
3. Move your lips noticeably.
4. Your teeth should never be kept closed while you are talking.
5. As your voice is the most direct expression of your innermost self, you should be careful to do yourself full justice with it.

Perhaps you've noticed the way people from other countries—friends, maybe, or actors in foreign movies—love the sound of their language. The French, Italians and English are especially devoted language lovers, vocally caressing

~~When You Speak~~

Speak

The way you listen is as revealing as a candid camera. You're sensitive, cultured, kind, cheerful. Your schooling is the most important part—you're basic—yet a part of you easily improved. You know how you sound.

A simple cut, an amusing cord. You surprise many people, sham a regional accent like the darling Southern girl with the high pitch because everyone's more attractive there. Girls spin into a shriek when you convey, by the sound of your voice, that your family comes from North, away. You want to sound like the people in your town, a perfect slur, their tongues sleepy and their lips lazy. Every day you condition the unappreciative to listen as if you might earn value.

Every word, every syllable, every sound must be given a chamber, with your teeth kept closed while you are talking—the most direct expression of your innermost self. You should be careful. They love the sound of their heritage, the slur and blur, the enclosure, a fault you will correct.

You'll find, as you practice in front of your mirror, that you look much prettier talking with a drawl. To-mah-to, to-may-to, tu-may-da. You think of others you could change, vocal fidgets, but colloquial speech loses its punch if you use it relentlessly. You're teased to the point of torture. You start talking in elaborate synonyms to make a point—*lady* instead of *woman*—incongruities, fantasies.

Contact. Well-bred. Gown. Pardon me. Permit me! Prior engagement. Sufficient.

Forget y'all.

15. When You Telephone

Talk with a stranger on the telephone and you conjure up a quick picture of the caller. If a voice sounds dull, mean, cross, overbearing—or friendly—you imagine a personality to match it. Your voice sketches your portrait and the one humming over the wires will surely be a pretty one if you use this trick: as you talk, pretend there's a mirror propped up in front of you. Are you smiling?

Do make certain that people can understand what you're saying—basic advice—and if friends often ask you to repeat what you've just said, check your voice and diction (see how on page 124). Or one of these foibles might be blighting your telephone personality:

- *mumbling* Speak up!
- *bellowing* Those miles of wire between you and the other person will do the amplifying. If you have a bad connection, make the call again or, if it's long distance, ask the operator if she can clear the line. Sometimes all you need to do is turn down the radio.
- *yatatayating* at supersonic speed—or drawling.
- *not talking into the mouthpiece* The telephone company has designed the instrument for perfect reception—and to what avail if you wave it off in space or hold it so close you deafen the listener?
- *drumming* absent-mindedly on the base of the instrument: it blurs what you're saying.
- *eating, drinking, cracking gum* while talking.

THE PHONE'S RINGING

Answer at home with a happy-sounding *hel-LO!* (*Smile* as you say that!) It's enough to make a boy stop calling if you mutter a dispirited, toneless *h'llo*. In a business office, you answer the phone with "Jones and Company; Miss Baker speaking" or "Mr. Giannini's office."

Suppose the caller asks for you.

Caller:	"May I please speak to Jane?"
You:	"Speaking." (rude, abrupt)
	"You're speaking to her." (even ruder)
	"Who's calling?" (*impossible*)
	"This is she." (sounds stiff)
	"This is Jane." (right)

~~When You Telephone~~

TONE

You conjure up cruelty, sketch it: the wires binding should demonstrate your value, so close it's like lust. It's enough to make a boy mutter toneless *h'llo*s. You like a rude, abrupt, impossible stiffness. You dream you make him want to bend. You trust the directed numbness; you allow it to identify yourself. You recognize that ancient game with a shudder, with a curt nod, like an adult. You use your last as well as your first choice: you lance the wound.

You call, "When will he be home, please? May I call then?" You cancel the call, "I'll wait."

You're a captive audience. You launch into a filibuster he has to interrupt: *I'm washing my hair.* That's embarrassing. Your monopolizing his time won't lengthen your privilege; your unbidden calls boring, without mission. It's harrowing as your messages—"I miss you!"—become gossip. That's typical; it's a habit, a void. The walls and woodwork of bones are scratch-pads—your rack of pride tallied on scars.

He makes the first move to cut short dating you; you take the cue, and flounder for an exit line. You say something like "I guess I'd better go," a spurn, building up courage, a lull in holding hands, over. Every minute is a tone unechoed. Polite white lies. He isn't waiting for a call.

You are, burning, the final words so little, worse than a hang-up (another way you really want him to hurt your heart) with a sort of response so vague and confused it's not rude. The trick is to pretend there are complicating circumstances, to translate his meanness to a spur-of-the-moment bad choice. You weigh lad against larder and decide you're a couch-warmer, preferring the sofa, popcorn. The boy is all kinds of misery. You commit yourself, brand yourself a social outcast: you lost him. You have your pride. Resurrect a second boy, a sweet boy who'll soothe your sour loss. You'd take a boy any time, any time, any time, any boy. You seek wariness, a boy sharp-tongued about your excessive interest—it pulls you, his distance, a regret you need.

But you sigh, track a date with the usual sort; attract an orderly, eager boy, more than you'd hoped. It's wise. It's perfectly proper. It's boring, being sure of the boy and his investment. You're sorry you can't care. You've made other plans already, you decline an invitation after accepting it, you do this for a good reason: you'd rather seek the sought. How trifling it seems, all those handouts for no effort.

You will probably be refused, but you want the stony silence. Your unfinished business is waiting, plaintive hellos into a silent instrument. He cannot come to the telephone. Or will not. The challenge is somehow an extension of interest—he must care enough to need to avoid gossip that you two may have been in touch. Carefully, slowly, like the thing in the world you'd hate most is to be a shame he'd rather not remember, you handle brief, firm humiliation and the conversation ends, laughter at the other end of the phone.

You quietly disconnect the depression. It is enough notice, that voice with a leer—indication you'll monitor as evidence that he's lit a little bulb on the switchboard: this girl is worth fucking with. That's familiar. That's what you want. The certainty you're a girl in a chrysalis, a moth trapped, this kind of desire.

16. Good Guestmanship

One of the nicest compliments is to be a guest: someone thinks enough of you to want to entertain you. Being a dinner guest or a house guest involves more formality than lunches, teas and parties with your friends—because grown members of a family are present.

HOW TO BE A DINNER GUEST

Suppose a boy asks you to dinner—on a Sunday, perhaps—to meet his family. You're delighted, of course, and possibly a bit edgy, because in a sense you will be on display. You want very much to be at ease and to be the kind of girl his mother expects her son to like. This guide will help you:

wear a simple, pretty dress; pumps; gloves—the same kind of clothes you'd wear to church on Sunday. Leave gloves, coat, hat, if you're wearing one, wherever you're told, but keep your bag with you if you like.

ask if you can help when your hostess heads for the kitchen after you've all talked awhile. "Could I do something, Mrs. Clark—carry in plates, perhaps? I'm used to helping my mother . . ." She may take you up on the offer or say, "Why don't you stay with Jack? He wants to show you his record collection." Do whatever she suggests. If she has no maid, offer some positive help during dinner: "Would you like me to take the dishes out, Mrs. Clark?" Some hostesses adore the friendliness of guests' helping; it makes others nervous.

before dinner some families serve sherry or cocktails, and often tomato or fruit juice will be passed too. "No, thank you" is the only answer you have to give if you don't care for anything.

when you go in to dinner wait till your hostess sits down before you take your place (which very likely will be on your host's right, unless there is another older woman present). If your hostess says to sit down and not wait for her, wait just long enough to give your beau or his father a chance to seat you.

a blessing is often asked, especially on Sunday, by the host or one of the younger children. Wait before starting to chat, until you're sure it won't be. Bow your head if it is, and you may murmur "amen" at the end. Quaker families say grace with all around the table joining hands, and some families belonging to other faiths have adopted this charming custom. Some families say grace after meals too.

~~Good Guestmanship~~
Good Guess

He meant to train you. Dinner at his house, family present; how to be appropriate + curb edges on display. You are the kind of girl his mother expects her son to like (simple, good, church-on-Sunday), but awkward with parents. You don't want to talk to them, nervous, "No thank you" the only answer you give. You don't care for anything but their son. They can tell.

You bow your head and you murmur, quiet, biding time, his teen-dark eyes much more appealing than anything on the plate. You wait till he's portioned out. You go through the motions. You're wise. You wait till you're asked. That's what he wants.

Your conflict? Principles. You excuse yourself to the bathroom, mother-watching. He's apprehensive about mistaking your signal as agency. You're playing the long game, a hurdle you'll evade through absenting your sexual arrival. You pose a problem to his canny kissing, you alarm him by pulling him against you—you needn't, but you must. The right girl wouldn't need physical evidence he wanted her after days of emailed pleasantries. Her beau would make plans to visit her. She'd like to meet the friends he kept in the life outside her. She'd check with him before saying she's a possession he owns. She would strip her fear fresh and neat, thank the mother, mind her modesty, and he would envelop her as he said he would. Later.

You are not the right girl.

No teen can pair a marred promise with all those other tricks that bring on trouble. Is it proper for a girl to visit a boy overnight? You know his parents will go to an early-evening party and leave the two of you to your own devices, that old opportunity to visit his Victorian cross-examination of your values.

You are left at the house a long, long time, just the two of you. It's after dark. It isn't a question of what you want, it's a matter of conventions. He is guarded, he won't admit it; you save the embarrassment of a good interruption. You can cash in later, should your beau offer. So you ask him to visit you. It's your prom, your theater. You act as if you're exactly what he steered. He's goaded into activity, amusement on the seat of your Taurus. You, definite about plans, guess his. He has other provisions for comfort, wants to go back paper-fresh. There are enough gutters, enough ash trays. This is a readable alarm clock.

He'll meet you one more time, a scrounge-up, sorry for you. You miss that you're unwanted, unbidden. You try to press against his neck but he leaves untouched. You sense nothing. He phones it in and you stay till he's left. Then you're left, a call at a distance, clean closure. Sure it's the key lime pie you didn't try, mother-weary, unavoidable, your urge to get his head in your legs costly. Sure you wouldn't have wanted to wait. If he'd tried. Sure.

17. Table Manners That Take You Anywhere

Any meal is a sociable occasion, and good table manners add to the sociability. The one magnificent reason for having them is so everyone can enjoy the food that's served. *Relaxed but thoughtful* is probably the key phrase that describes the kind of person you like to eat with. Most of the rules have been dinned at you since you were bib age, but constant repetition may have dulled some of the points, so perhaps a review is in order:

- Wait till a few others have been served before starting. When you're a guest, take your cue from your hostess; some families say grace before a meal. Mind her, though, if she says go ahead and don't wait for her.
- *A napkin* goes on your lap unless you tuck it under your chin at a spaghetti or lobster feast. When you leave the table, deposit it at the left side of your plate; the only time you fold it is when you're given a napkin ring.
- You sit up straight, with the chair pulled in to the table. You'll look better and the food won't dribble on your clothes or the floor.
- *Elbows* are fine on the table—occasionally—except when you have food or eating implements in hand.
- *Fidgeting* spoils the appetite (the other fellow's). Stop it if you find you're carving patterns on the tablecloth with a fork, fiddling with the silver or running a finger idly around the rim of your glass.
- If you're not sure *which fork* to use, eye your hostess. Most tables have the silver set from the outside in, toward the plate, in the order in which it will be needed. Many restaurants put every piece of silver they can find at each place; that's when you have to take your chances. Most people will just think you're absent-minded if you take the wrong implement.
- Food stays pretty much at plate level until you're ready to put it in your mouth. Hold bread close to the butter plate when you break and butter it.
- *Elbows* stay at table level even if the meat is tough to cut.
- You *don't reach* across anyone else's place. "May I have the salt, please?" is the way to get it.
- *If you drop* an implement, leave it on the floor until the meal is over. If you're in a restaurant, you don't pick it up at all.
- *Any glass* with a stem is held by the bowl for better balance. Otherwise it might wobble and spill.
- It's a nice idea to pat your mouth with a tissue before drinking out of a glass: it avoids unaesthetic smudges.

~~Table Manners That Take You Anywhere~~
Take You Anywhere

A sociable boy, the one magnificent reason to force the person you have been since you were bib-age to face your fear: a meal with a napkin on your lap.

(You tuck it under your chin, a spaghetti feast at home)

You're given a napkin ring, you sit up straight, the chair pulled in.

(You look bad, the food-dribble on your clothes, elbows on the table)

You fidget, a petite flit of patterns on the tablecloth with a fork, fiddling with the silver, a finger 'round the rim of your glass. You're not sure which fork to use—that old trope—you have to take your chance with your absent date in the loo. Pick both.

You don't reach anyone's hopes; you don't pick up at all. You won't avoid unaesthetic smudges. The long trial, the spoon in the glass you forget, jab your eye, soup slurped, teeth clicked with spoons. Only puppies are cute smacking their food.

Some people do. Some people don't answer a question. Your mouth is full, unmanageable: a look at a toddler, not a teen. Nerves, your nerves. You need to corral stray breaths on the blade of a knife, removing the uneatable from your mouth; prune the pits, bones, slivers of doubt with your fingers. You can't retire behind your napkin for any of these maneuvers.

Choking? Leave the table till a platter doesn't splatter the fraction of elegance you've shown him, enticing trust in your fitness by his side. Convince him, soup to spoon, you fit the bill—a girl who can transcend her lack of opportunities and model the decorum he wants.

So you eat steamed clams, pop the whole thing in your mouth, fake-swallow, vomiting in your napkin when he looks the other way. You aren't as skillful as you suppose. You don't get flustered, a slippery peasant, when corn-on-the-cob is on the table. You glide it between your teeth, scraped cobs at your fingertips. Preferring mozzarella sticks to kale kills your cred.

It won't happen; you've narrowed his vision to your soured cream. You reach, a gesture as sloppy as half-price nachos at Applebee's.

18. For Men Only

Men are nice to have around—and if you're not absolutely certain of this, just watch the girls' faces light up when an attractive boy joins the group. An attractive boy can be tall and thin, short and thin, tall and husky, short and husky. It isn't a way of looking that makes him attractive—it's because his manners are those of a gentleman. You can tell because he

- stands up promptly when a girl, a grown woman or an older man comes into the room or crosses it to talk with him
- opens doors for such people and steps back to let them through first
- is the last to get in a car and the first to get out
- carries parcels for ladies of any age (not packages that look too feminine or a handbag; besides, no sensible girl would let him)
- says "sir" to older men
- gives up his seat on the bus or subway to someone who needs it (not necessarily to a pretty girl who is perfectly able to stand—unless she is holding a baby, looks as though she will be shortly or is carrying a large rubber plant)
- never uses a small courtesy—picking up a package or a glove—as a wedge for starting a conversation with a girl in public places, such as the subway and the movies
- helps a lady remove her coat in a restaurant, movie, theater, church—and hangs it up or checks it, if necessary
- leads a girl to a restaurant table and pulls back her chair—or, in a more formal restaurant, lets the girl follow the captain, who will pull out her chair
- gives the order to the waiter or waitress (or captain) after asking the lady what she would like; he gives her choices first for each course, and this makes serving the meal smoother for all. (More about restaurant behavior on page 85.)

Attractive men know all the complimentary customs, the little extras that make a girl feel attractive, too. (Actually this being attractive is as "catching" as the common cold—now referred to as a virus—and it certainly raises the happiness level.) The attractive boy knows how to say hello; he smiles, shakes hands firmly, doesn't fuss about taking off his glove if the delay would make matters awkward. When he passes a girl he knows on the street, he touches his hat in a sort of half-salute. If he stops to talk, he takes it off (not by the brim but by pinching the crown and lifting the hat off). The hat also comes off in an apartment-house elevator, when he's introduced, or talking to any older person. The hat stays on in office elevators, lobbies and halls, such public buildings as post offices, terminals, stores.

~~For Men Only~~

For Me Only

Men need—if you're not absolutely certain of this, just watch their faces light up—an attractive jealousy, a husky way of looking at the one they want. Men are last to get in and the first to escape a sensible girl; they need a pretty girl, because desire's a sham. Scarcity leads a girl to present her value first-face: her unavailability.

A boy says *mine*—"love" would make matters awkward. He passes a girl he knows; he touches his hat in a sort of half-salute. He stops to talk. He's a free agent. You choose to respect his walk, a low nod with a little shoulder action, but not the claw, the lock.

He's a male, an automatic king. He doesn't scurry to the curb every time a girl's streetside, yet he doesn't cuddle arm-in-arm, your elbow a rudder to steer him back. You don't mind, but he doesn't take off his jacket when he's visiting. He's holding someone else; she's putting the sofa cushions on the floor in his fantasy, spontaneous lust you don't use.

He's near the end of his list with you, her busy signal a siren he can't avoid.

He suggests the movies, or whatever. Most girls hesitate, but you like the idea of date after date after date in public places, want to show off your impatient, wandering prize. *Me, mark me, notice as he buys the tickets smoothly, matter-of-factly*; he treats me but doesn't bring flowers. He stays safe on the matter. You're tall and casual; she's little and pins flowers to her bag.

He brings her into the conversation, a duty—his mother's best friend's daughter!—and he's as nice to her as he would be to a girl he really liked. It's his hand on a post, a path. She's taken, and he waits at a prearranged spot; he goes to do things he "never" does for a very good reason: conquest. You'd never brainwash or force—can't discourage a determined boy.

It's humiliating to be honest about it. Men will chase girls. If he doesn't catch you now, he'll find another. You go out on a date to break the impression you created; men don't change as fast as girls do when faded beauty wears out. Attraction for action's what all of them want. To believe in change? Problematic. So: a dance, a party, you dress to make men cum. He will have times of favor. You order, imperious, intent on some strong, masculine threat. Some men need to lose a bet. This is very important to remember when you're bluffing.

You cajole a boy to touch you, your arm bent at the point where he joins yours, aroused straight from the hips, just the trim for effect. He slides his date to service you, mocking her, attentive. But you're a removable resource, Occam's heuristic, the next pick.

19. Tips About Tipping

There's only one rule to learn about tipping—and that's to ask someone who knows the community and its customs. Your parents when you're at home, your hostess when you're visiting, a well-informed friend who's lived a number of years in a place that's new to you. Not only the amount you tip but also *whom* you tip may differ from town to town and from shop to shop in the same town.

Why tip? For three reasons, at least—as a mark of appreciation of good service, because the tip is an expected part of a service employee's weekly earnings, and to make sure you will continue to get good service. Knowing how to tip makes you more a part of the grown-up world. Since you are young, no one will expect you to tip as generously as an older person; your nice smile and polite thank-you will make the amount you tip acceptable.

Here is a check list of situations where you may be expected to tip and probable amounts. Do check the tipping customs where you are to make the suggestions accurate for you.

DELIVERY SERVICE

supermarket	No tip. You pay a fixed amount for delivery when you pay your tab, but you tip a boy if he carries large bags of items to your car.
laundry	No tip
department store	No tip. Unless a parcel is delivered as a special service—perhaps in bad weather—by an employee not hired to deliver packages

CHECKROOM SERVICE

	10¢ to 25¢, depending on the quality of the place. At a hotel or top restaurant, 25¢. At a skating rink, 10¢—unless you are checking many bundles, an umbrella and schoolbooks in addition to your coat; if so, 25¢

Tip

There's only one rule to learn about the coy customs of men: numb a place before he can. Evade ploys + yearning to make sure you will stay apart. You're young; no one expects generosity in your actions. You ice him out, a suggestion from a movie, because resolve's a runny mess if you're too close to the heat of a bruise, a throb that fascinates, straightening out a mistake you let happen to prove it burns.

Hit me baby one more time. You smother, gas on.

20. The Ins And Outs Of Fashion

Fashion—the art of personal appearance, the knack of having style or clothes sense, of knowing how to dress—is a skill some are blessed with, others have to study and practice to achieve it. It's easier to understand fashion if you think of it as being remarkably like understanding boys: both are unpredictable, positive, changeable, charming, indispensable—with a lot of rock-solid strength underneath the surface. As your taste and judgment become surer, you realize that the kinds of clothes you like fall into a pattern that suits your particular life.

You don't like every boy, you don't like every style—just the one that suits you. When you discover the strength underneath the whims of fashion, you can be decisive about what is best for you.

What makes for a strong fashion sense?

- *having a sense of style,* a willingness to accept the current and the new *within the limits* of what's becoming to you. Example: a full-swinging coat that foreshortens arms and legs if you are small—so you get a flared coat that gives the effect of the full coat within your dimensions.
- *recognizing what is in good taste* and pleases the eye, whether the wearer is standing, sitting or moving. Examples: you like a sweater that fits easily instead of one you bulge in. The dress or skirt you buy has a gentle swing; it doesn't cling to your thighs, ride up or wrinkle when you walk or sit.
- *being individual,* catering to your own special likes. Example: you wear a pale-blue belt with a navy dress instead of the obvious red one. You team a sherbet-colored sweater—orange, lemon or lime—with a beige dress instead of the expected red, white or blue.
- *learning to dress for yourself* instead of just for special occasions or special people. As a young teen-ager, I had a crush on a sophisticated older woman who was a friend of my family's. I admired her very much and was embarrassed one day to discover she had come to lunch—and there I was, looking very scraggly and badly put together. I mumbled something about being sorry to look so awful when she was there, and she said gently, "You should always be well groomed *for yourself.*" Her words made a great impression on me, and I have learned that dressing for myself, trying always to look my best—whether I'm at work, going to a dance or digging in the garden—adds immeasurably to the self-confidence and inner serenity that make for happy living.
- *wearing the right thing at the right time.* Example: you take a small bag on a date and save the larger one for your trip on the jet. You never wear

Out of Fashion

The art of appearance, the knack of knowing how to kill with a dress—it's like a boy: predictable, changeable, indispensable. A lock. Underneath the surface, you judge your zeal. You like a pattern; you don't like every boy. You like everyone you discover straining against the current. You form a sieve, recognizing who pleases the eye, who fits easily in the skirt you cling to your thighs, wrinkling your morals, so obvious, so expected.

Once, you had a crush on a sophisticated older man—a fiendish embarrassment, a scraggly, badly-put-together mumblement when he said, gently, *you shouldn't always look so self-aware.* Right? At the time you agreed, scared in a sweater, schoolish, ashen. You needed the cliff, what it would mean to hew a look. You wear shorts and you know you look terrible in them with your thin legs, baggy around the ass.

You're as young as you will ever be; you're as lonely, hovering close to violation (proof, part of being female). Some conduct holds true: it's better to be under than over, it's better to be carelessly deeding a way in, anywhere, anytime. But choose.

You squiggle, short-waisted, your tiny and misshapen size; you pant until you fit properly, neat pleats. You collate

Girl Look: it makes boys want to take care of you with those cellophane hands. Femme-Fatale Look scares boys. The Girl Kit makes boys comfortable: dresses, skirts, teeter-totter heels, festoons of pearls, the fem embedded. Emphasized. A rattle, a ban on corduroy's kneecap clap blocking his grip.

You wear more jewelry, a velvet bow, a barrette, your hair softer and perfumed, cascading. You wouldn't wear it for yourself. You veer toward success, verging close to glee at how simple it is. You wash out your hosiery, buy some millinery, shovel up the most smashing dress you can find, Cinderella-shift out the door a brand new girl, certain you enchant the minute you leave home. Practice stooping, sitting, rising. In case.

So, sure. A buddy at the last dance, a damaging diss, a clean kid shunt. Your silly teenage tack mashed, no match or complement. You were ashamed to watch the effect of the soiled, grubby vintage t-shirt you thought was cool. You're in a more adult world now; you loused that up. A switch, you go all out with frills, leaving behind what you need to accommodate the item you want: appeal.

You pack away your discomfiting androgyny because you can't compete with Kate Moss. Even she has real breasts—a feral mark of respect you envy, that lag between childhood and being grown up—an urge you drown, you can't live without but you will have to live without. You obscure little lumps (a way of life). You choose the right size; you don't need very big ones. Soft pouches look reasonable.

You clutch tissues when the pressure's on; stuffing has a tranquilizing effect, dissociating appearance from your essential, ruinous truth.

He wakens a sinew, a cluttered muscle you'll build. You need strong will. Protect your yes—it marks you as a player, sharp, a cardshark at love. You bag up personas like a gymnast's floor routine, eclectic performances of sexual knowledge. There is an inverse snobbism: the less grasped, the tighter gripped.

The frontier stretches, a stockade vexing your breached past—so close to satisfaction, but you look like a department-store mannequin, fancy, removed, pure. You skid across the ice, hands out; you implore (considered in poor taste), trying to brake to no avail, head over heels. So show off your figure, make a neon display of immodesty—most boys like to whistle at three inches of bikini, red about the ears and particularly at the crotch. You bend over; sure, you can play at pantomiming. You better do it, because things like girls are nonreturnable. Beware of the bra, that bone, obviously too big for you; it will only make you look ready.

A final evening, crazed by daylight wisps *you* cracked, sworn outside of love to make a ring fit; the stone *you* threw, the dazed droop when it didn't detach. You couldn't. You handle such effects oddly, junking the whole endeavor. The count rolls on; you cover your head, wailing. Who can you shake out of your folds? What remains to be done? When?

Cycles are a basic part of attractiveness. You put anything back in your closet that looks sexy. You do a quick repair job, a fluid removal, a total immersion, dipped and dried. You choose to mend matters before it's too late: the bold reinforcement of girlishness around your ass, wound tight; a wink, a quick pressure until he sees, cream-mellow, the ethereal hint he loves. Your innocence needs coddling to combat ripping; he's the suave one brushing in the same direction, rubbing gently. You'll be turned head to foot, a try-out. Your wedding or a funeral.

But you're free as can be; you wear a headband of flowers instead of a suitable corona. If you're going to be a girl, you'll be the kind you like best: natural, singsong, childish, aware that your cover covers nothing. You dream of a lock without a key, of swearing the oaths of a man. When he calls for you, you will shut your hole; a small power, a way to tell them.

21. Presents That Are Perfect

Starting with the tie rack you made for father as a child, you've probably loved the whole idea of presents and the fun of deciding what to give people you love. Not that there aren't some perplexing moments mixed in with the fun: if you're short of money, the right thing may be harder to find. Choosing a present for a boy may be difficult because you want it to be so perfect. The first wedding presents you buy may cause you a worry or two about your own taste in this very formal moment of decision. Or maybe the question is whether you should give a present at all. And then there is the perplexity of the present you're not quite sure you should keep. The time-tested rules about presents are these:

1. You don't give a present that would embarrass the one you're giving it to. Embarrassment can be caused by a present that's obviously too expensive:
   - The friend might be distressed that you'd spent far more than you could afford.
   - If the occasion were an exchange of Christmas presents, the friend might be unhappy because your present made hers (or his) look insignificant.
   - The friend might have a much smaller allowance than you and be hurt to have the difference underlined by your Lady-Bountiful contribution —even if it's skis or a sweater set you know she longs to have. (The best you can do here is to give her yours—you get new skis from your family —or say you know the color of the sweater set is her favorite blue.)

Or embarrassment can be caused by a present that's too personal:

- A boy might think that you were taking the romance too seriously or that he'd given you the idea that he was taking it more seriously than he actually is.
- A boy might not want others—his family, friends—to think you two were close enough to justify a very personal present—such as a sports jacket; a suit; underwear; jewelry; any present with a double meaning; books or records with amorous titles and tasteless contents; anything engraved, printed or embroidered that might give an outsider a poor impression; or any message you write inside a book which might be innocent enough when explained—"Darling, I'll never forget our wonderful night at the Middletown-Hilton! All my love always, Sue" (which merely means the fraternity dance when he finally got around to pinning Sue—but just think what his Aunt Hilda could make out of that inscription without the explanation!)

~~Presents That Are Perfect~~

Present Perfect

The track you have trod to love, the perplexing road to find a boy, a wedding, a worry about your formal moment of decision—or maybe the question is whether you've seen the present you're not quite sure you'd keep. Buried beneath courtesies, you made significant allowances for failures caused by restraint. You take romance seriously. He'd given you the idea. He was taking it seriously.

He might want his friends to think you're closer. You represent a double meaning, amorous titles and tasteless contents in every message you write; innocent when explained, a code to make out, but he never tries his key. You'd like something he has no right to give—you'd give him anything. He sees you in black lingerie. He's uncertain, the decision division tucking the resentment he might have felt beneath confidence. It will be remembered hazily, your attempts to make him make you. You will be embarrassed—*is it that hard?*—on his birthday. You haven't known him long, you give him your heart in your breast, rushing him, heavily; you have sex-need thick on the tongue. He could taste it, but he won't.

But neither do you ask for it, or hint, too shy to ask outright, a sentimentalization dying to defeat the purpose of keeping your face before him. He'd say he doesn't want to go there too soon; you have plenty of time, hugging your shoulders, a chummy slough-gesture he couldn't resist to remind you he's glad to end the exchange if you can't. You might like to give up; you would be willing to leave his quaver and concern (it isn't necessary). You'll probably feel dreadful if you don't tell him to grip your hipbone instead of the grating squeeze of his thumb against yours but, porcelain-clean, wipe need off your mind.

Having broken a promise, it might be nice to imagine yourself into the future he desires: the shuddering one without desire. You're struggling to look delighted, six rose-sprigged petticoats padding your consecrated and blessed bride-wet longing. When you stand to embrace him, the moisture evaporates. You are reluctant to give up love's gilt, the usual trappings.

A flame holds snapshots—and the negatives. An eye-dart, a hand in your lap, an arched back, but they're all yours. Portraits of a girl, plastic and slick and distinctly composed, a great moral-raiser, a representation-you. He might not marry you if you can't inhabit the ideal. Men say what they want, and there you are, absentmindedly holding your pubic bone, blank for inspiration.

He might notice. He might not. He sees the definition that's caught his fancy, the dictionaried rule-book, a tumbler filled with #2 pencils and a girl standing beside it, ready to take dictation, neat and pert in her plaid on the side, a blushing beauty, rows of rickrack curls, camera-ready. She's the best of all the world's girls: eager, a spayed switch-hitter, permanent, patient.

It's nearly decision-time, his hand out, a small velvet vow, parching.

22. The ABC's Of Letters

Mail call—at home, at school, in the Army—is a highlight of the day. Letters bring news, give you a chance to visit with a friend. They bring pleasure . . . in a birthday card, a clipping that makes you laugh, an invitation. Letters carry messages, send reminders, give thanks, do errands and even patch up quarrels. Many of them are treasured over the years, to be read and reread as they keep the memories of happy times alive.

Each letter is a bit of your own personality put on paper: you want it to picture what you are really like as it accomplishes its purpose. In the pages that follow, you'll find ways to write letters, what to put in them and what to put the message on—plus the basic rules of letter-writing. Equally important (and more fun), you'll find ways to make your letters as individual as you are.

WHAT WILL YOU SAY?

Most people love to write newsy, everyday letters; others, although they can spend hours on the telephone talking with a friend, go blank when they must *write.*

You may wail, "I have nothing to write!" But a friend who recently moved away or is out of town for the summer is as interested that you have gained five pounds or have a new beau as if she were still around the corner. Write about what happened yesterday, books you've read, movies you've seen, ideas you've had. Add clippings of interest to you both, such as the announcement of a friend's wedding snipped from the local paper. Or join with the crowd in writing a "round robin" letter to which everyone contributes a paragraph.

Be spontaneous about letters. If the reason you're writing Susie is to tell her "I've been accepted at college!" don't ruin the effect by starting the letter with a trite "The weather is lovely here today." Feel free to use contractions, such as "I'm" and "you're" . . . but never use faulty grammar. Happily, most of you can write lively letters.

If you must write bad news, do it with tact and good sense. Prevent worry by telling no more than you must and no less. If you write, "Hugh was in a terrible automobile accident" without adding that he escaped with minor cuts, you could make your reader frantic. Want to pour your sorrows into the ear of a trusted friend? It's usually wiser not to, but if you must get your feelings down on paper, do so—then tear up the paper or wait a day or two and read it again before mailing it. If you send it, your problems may vanish—to remain only in the worried mind of your friend. Keep *all* touchy letters overnight before mailing them, to judge, later, whether you really meant every word you wrote.

It's a thoughtful habit to write not only when you have news to relay or a

~~The ABC's of Letters~~
Fetters

Each letter is a chance to win him over. A reminder, an errand, a quarrel over the years, read and reread, the memories alive—you put on paper a picture to accomplish its purpose: indelibility, words you haven't spoken. You didn't think. You'd been wed, an elaborate pantomime, once.

(Tell no more than you must)

You write minor truths to get your feelings down, hiding them in lyrics. You really mean every word—a thoughtful relay, a baton—expecting he does too, promises shy and obscure. You're searching furiously for pages that never existed. You would say, if you were "talking," nothing. Or the obvious: you love him. You want to swear undying devotion when he is really accepting little more than friendship.

His distance drives your drop, the cowardly consideration—he lives in another town—his reason. *It's really hard to keep up a long-distance romance.*

Sometimes a spasmodic correspondence can be left to die, but it's been heavy. You're ashamed you sent so much. He fibs with a brief, non-emotional note, and he doesn't send a Christmas card. You nudge him to react—you know he's a bad correspondent—and you write to his friend, so casual behind your laser focus she doesn't see the formula, a prompt visit "spontaneously" offered to her new bestie. Your overnight bag is full of the words you'll shove in his mouth, blobs of sentiment you'll give him to chew to kick-start his salivary gland.

(Lovelines used to dribble out on their own; they've dried to form acknowledgments)

He is no more effusive in-person than he was on the page, his mien stiff and inadequate—or trussed in nervous, hopelessly old-fashioned Darcian regrets. You tolerate the charade as proof he is still searching for the right words to retract. You will abide.

You will never see him again. But you will see him again, his name folded in a letter, another email written with great care, a song-lyrics-ricochet indicating a certain amount of effort, that literary construction which allowed interpretation but provided an excuse. It suits. It will leave no doubt in your mind as to what the next move should be.

You scour liner notes; you put your own restraint on the page, cutting off the campaign right before confessing. You can do that too. You like the question, not the answer—they bind, they trap, they leave no openings. It is the hint betrayed in the address, the enveloped interest sealed in the contact.

He knows that you read between the lines.

23. Getting Along Successfully In A Job

Your family has just given their consent for you to look for a job—the most exciting news you've had in a long time. The word gets around, and your friends' question-for-the-day is "Are you really going to work?" Are you? Will you be one of those young people whose interest in a job is equally divided between the money and the fringe benefits—the kind one employment director describes as "just a body at a desk"? Or are you going to work? Are you eager to do a good job and to learn to do a bigger one? Will you be businesslike about business?

If the answers to the last three questions above are "yes," you're the kind of employee that companies want. They can't promote machines—only people. While you may not be planning on a lifetime business career, the years you do work can be very rewarding. You'll be proud of the progress you make, the interests and skills you develop; perhaps one day you'll be proud that your business ability has helped pay the way for your husband to finish law school.

Finding a job It helps if you have learned your lessons in school before you apply. You need to *know* arithmetic, grammar, spelling, punctuation. It helps a great deal if you have learned to type (a minimum of 30 words a minute is required for a beginner's job) and maybe to use a simple computing machine. If your high school doesn't include these last two courses in the curriculum, you might make one or both a summer project or, if your schoolwork permits, go to a business school after classes. Have your Social Security card and résumé ready to take with you on your job hunt. Never made a résumé? Most firms ask to see this brief typewritten history of your life when you apply for a job; sometimes a firm keeps the résumé, so it's a good idea to have several carbon copies. These are the facts you put in:

- your name, address and telephone number
- the date and place of your birth
- your Social Security number
- your typing speed
- the names and addresses of the schools you've gone to
- any course, academic or commercial, which might have some tie-in with the job you're applying for
- extracurricular activities, if they are pertinent: school paper, yes; sophomore hazing committee, no; captain of the tennis team, yes
- previous jobs—summer, part-time, even baby-sitting, if you've gone to one family for a year or more. Give the names, addresses and telephone num-

~~Getting Along Successfully in a Job~~

A Lull, A Job

Sixteen and legal, no fringe benefits—no one debutantes anymore, no hemline ushering boys into husbands. You have learned your lessons. You know the cook feeds on sublimation, but the governess gets the widower. Your mission is the job you might be able to get if you put your number on the first page—any role that puts you in front of men. Drugstore checkout girl, waitress, secretary. Clean fingernails to show you're not desperate. You'll stand out if you're conservative in your approach, a sweet helpmeet apt to giggle. One bold act men can't immediately sort out is whether you're laughing at them, or at your own presumption that they noticed you. You get to work.

You dole out donuts and cigarettes, shoveling pastry cream into the trash with a college boy who does not try to take advantage, his half-smile pleasantries. He should know a girl like you ought to get married and have a home and children by twenty-three, though he won't help provide for retirement. You think about it overnight, agreeably and simply turn in your apron, and fill out another application.

You interface with fathers as a learning center receptionist—a mistake, miscalculating how many boys sign up for SAT prep—so you try to see them as practice, a flash into your lipsticked future. Plenty of time to conduct an office romance with your pert pencil skirt and attentive swivel when the door chimes, but the men are looking past you at their children, fear locked on their futures. You should not be expected to tackle this kind of problem. You want to grow up and get your pension. You want the insurance. You want to know a boy might date you. Then promote you.

24. The Formalities Of Life

Some of the events and milestones of living are marked by ceremonies that are stately, dignified and carefully planned. They are often very beautiful to see and hear, and they are *always* packed with protocol. This briefing will help you know what takes place and what will be expected of you.

BANQUETS

You just might find yourself attending a large public dinner or banquet. Your usual good restaurant manners will stand you in good stead here. A few added tips:

- There will be no one to seat you, so just walk to the table assigned to you. Sit down, introduce yourself, and chat pleasantly with your tablemates. If no table is assigned, join a congenial-looking group already seated, asking first, "May I sit here?" Ask "Is this seat taken?" before you claim it. (Whenever you *are* assigned a table, stay at it. Switching from an assigned table confuses the banquet committee.)
- Service at banquets is often hurried so that there will be time for speeches or a stage presentation. Co-operate by refraining from asking the waiter for special services. If a fruit cocktail is placed before you and you don't happen to like fruit cocktail, leave it on your plate. The waiter will remove it when he brings the next course. However, if your religion says it's a fish day and only meat is served, you may ask the waiter for a substitute. Hotels and restaurants catering banquets are prepared for this and always have fish or eggs ready.
- The "distinguished guests" at the speakers' table or on the dais (raised platform at one end of the room) are sometimes seated after everyone else. When this is the case, one often rises and remains standing until these guests have been seated. However, this may not be expected at the banquet you attend, so watch other tables for your cue. If a clergyman is at the speakers' table, he may be called on to say grace before dinner. Stand (if others are doing so) and bow your head.
- If the toastmaster has a list of names of "distinguished guests and committee chairmen who did so much to make this dinner a success" and requests that you "please hold your applause until I have finished reading," please do so.
- Silence, please, during the speeches or entertainment—except, of course, for laughter where it is indicated.
- And please hear the speeches out. If you must leave before the program is over, do it between speeches or acts, while the group is still applauding.

~~The Formalities of Life~~

The Formal Lie

Meted tone, slivered by ceremony, dignified and carefully planned tests packed with protocol, briefing what takes place and what will be expected of you. You'd been mannering steadily, warmed up on Austen's teens, that spectacle of delicate remove. When the course has been charted and proven navigable, you don't question the era-specific acts, the grappling grotesquerie. A girl without a history invents her education, so you predict a return to gentle, courtly love: church parties, conventional dances, coming-out presentations. You prepare accordingly.

Edwardian daughters met eligible sons intending dynasties, the bleakness of being a maiden aunt graying over their shoulders. You note the boys called "Trey," setting your sights on the younger brother, the easier prey. He won't demand a girl better with his mother than all the debs of the season; the duty can be accomplished with other clingers to the family fortune. You stomach grande dame condescension poorly, your Midwestern mother's full-hearted hugs nothing like the cold, society *how-do-you-dos* of Wharton's van der Luydens, curt nods til you get the cue.

The ribbon holding your hair is green rather than blue, little mistakes, misreads. All the hours you spend, Forsytes in hand, poring over their unwise men—you miss the candles being swapped for a light bulb, too entrenched in afternoon dresses to remember corsets were cut an eon ago.

Certain society has stressed the conviction that commitment to the past is crucial; a girl investigates all means to insure success. The policies eliminate the need for guessing at a boy's intentions: the language of flowers is clear that a fistful of rosebuds and moss means "a confession of love." Your box of violets never arrives, but you don't require Gilbert's lilies, content to wait for perfection, Anne-ish.

In the interim, practicing calligraphic witticism for your future correspondences, you study love, dissecting confession and the way it can unfurl slowly, like a fan, securing a husband with a flirtatious snap. You learn measure and meter, how to appear in demand and keep a boy on a string—nouns omitted, just to be safe—waiting for your invitation.

You plan to drink champagne in coupes, delicate sips, a bit of wedding cake under your pillow. The one you dream of is supposed to be the one you will marry. It's an old custom, the bride and her bouquet, a decorous grasp at tradition, the frou-frou frothing action proudly unnerving any restraint you have learned. Afternoon "at-homes," waiting for a caller in the sitting room, formal with your hands attentively hovering by the caddy—*lemon? milk?*—as the tea overstews, goes cold. Prom looming, your fear clears, metabolizes. The wrench of want an exception, you arrange your own escort and anticipate your entrance, arm safe within his, nosegay in hand, your gilt-edged dance card imminent.

But your prom's theme is "Willy Wonka." Freshmen in Oompa-Loompa costumes wave you through as he takes control of your hips, grinding to Ginuwine. You follow, hesitant at first, but compliance is expected. That much is familiar. Your new education begins, a crash-land, your dignity waylaid, abandoned.

25. P.S. For The Future: YOUR ENGAGEMENT, YOUR WEDDING

Although you know all about being a guest at a wedding by now, the day will come when you star at your own, and what you will want to know is somewhat different. Your wedding should be consistent with your way of life. Very likely your family will give you any kind you set your heart on—and the choice you make may be the greatest test of your good manners that you'll ever face. Out of kindness to your family, ask for one that is appropriate to the way you live, to your religious beliefs and to your father's income. A wedding is no time to be incongruous. It *is* incongruous for two church members to be married in the city hall or for a family that lives in a modest house with one six-year-old car to have a wedding reception for 300 guests at the country club. It's incongruous to order engraved wedding invitations when you could have the less expensive thermographed ones and fill out your empty hope chest with the sheets and pillowcases you really need. It's probably just as incongruous for you to hold out for a small wedding in the chapel, followed by lunch for the two families, when your mother has the time, money and energy to give you a lavish wedding and your father has his heart set on a big splurge for his only daughter. Do remember that the biggest or the smallest wedding can be equally memorable. A bride can be as beautiful in a pretty pastel suit or in a wedding dress she's made herself as in fifty yards of pearl-embroidered pure silk costing hundreds of dollars. A reception at home may not be as grand as the one your cousin Alison had at the country club, but it might be much warmer and more affectionate.

The details of a lovely wedding are the same; the degrees of formality, elaborateness and expense vary a great deal. In the pages that follow, you will find many details and many variations; choose the ones that will be appropriate—and therefore in the best taste—for your own wedding plans. You'll add to everyone's happiness if you do.

YOUR ENGAGEMENT

Telling the families After you've said "yes," the first thing you and your fiancé should do is tell your respective parents.

- Your father may want to "have a chat with that young man" and vice versa. This isn't as Victorian as it sounds. Both men are deeply, vitally concerned with your future. It's better that they discuss it frankly than leave their questions unasked and unanswered. Leave your father and fiancé alone as they talk. If possible, get out of the house (and take your mother with you!). But come back at a prearranged time, perhaps an hour or two later, to rescue them.

~~P.S. For the Future: Your Engagement, Your Wedding~~
Forth, Future

The day will come when you will want to know if you've failed the greatest test of girlhood: did you gather wool, or fill your hope chest with enough bride material? All your machinations mean nothing if you haven't hooked a fiancé. A noisy tick, a primal certainty that your wasp's nest will not survive the summer—wasn't so many centuries ago that a woman's life expectancy crumbled into bits by thirty, all those premenopausal eggs buried alive. Your daughters are scratching at their coffins, screaming to be born; your grandparents refuse to nestle into theirs until they can rest sure someone will inherit their DNA. That's the way it's done.

You can't fail your ancestral lessons; there's a coding you can't reproduce if you don't trip the right wire. A girl is a bride, a bride is a wife, a wife is a mother, and that's how you'll get your girls, because women do it the hard way. You cannot crack your rib cage open, stoically re-gluing the bones together in a cinched corset, if you do not have daughters circled around like an old-time medical theater: *watch this, pay attention, this is how it hurts.* Kissing your fingertips, making a cross over your ovaries, you bless them to sleep.

Now, about that wedding. It's a simple script, which is

often the least attainable when you're still simple. Age complicates appeal; he'll finally be ready to accept afternoons shuttling the kids to activities if you can wait for his libido to slow, but your need is too urgent. Better to demur—*we can have them whenever we're ready*—than to accommodate the old bachelor-til-forty saw. You need a man to stuff cotton in the seams before the threads disintegrate. A lily-white lie, a necessary omission, a word about frayed nerves you can't calm: estrogen. Elasticity boomerangs your womb each month, pheromones you observe, direct, control. You wait to ovulate and then you wait, limbs loosened in a shrug exactly like a screen siren, a woman who wears her own right-hand-ring.

Nothing makes a man stiffen into decision like a woman who doesn't watch; a ruse old, new, borrowed. Something blue is cupped in your palm but there's no release until you've got his last name. You groom in strokes, emphasizing the duties of a partner, the availability, reaching for the brass ring in his pocket. If you do it right, he hands it over in a trance, mouthing the right words, an automaton you can control.

Open the binder to pick your trousseau, your wife-wear—this is the moment to change your scissored-and-saved fantasies into a corporeal presence. Your actions swift, concentrated—as if you've been planning this your whole life—you activate Fiancée Mode, ostentatiously posing in lingerie on the bed to remind him of what awaits. The groom gives his bride jewelry; she may give him anything but the trump card. It's supposed to be bad luck for the bride to rehearse her own victory. You finish preparations, make a friend swear to grip his arm at the church-front 'til you get him. From now on you will be a man's. You want to savor this last little-girl moment.

The years of insufficiency wash over you; the teen terror of loneliness a stain no marriage license can cleanse. He might leave you, but he's going to leave someone else behind. You wind your mother's veil around a bouquet, a tight tulle holding your nature together, striding up the aisle without your glasses on, vague nods to the faces flanking the plank, focusing on the clarity standing before you: his hands clasped over the genitals that will grant you your curly-haired little possibilities. You dream of collecting them like chronicles, a fresh diary every two years, elbowing the etiquette guides off your shelf. But you're still staring at the test, pencil poised, when the period ends.

26. A Treasury Of Entertaining Ideas

everything about parties . . . food, fun, games, table setting and all the trimmings . . . what to say from the first invitation to the last good-by

INVITATIONS

There are about as many ways to invite people to a party as there are kinds of parties.

You may give your invitations in person, by telephone, by writing little notes, by sending cards you either make or buy. If you have folded visiting cards called "informals," you may use them. When you ask anyone in person or by telephone, it's a good idea to follow up the invitation with a reminder.

The important thing is to include all the information in your invitation—the date, the time to come and your name and address.

Plus extra information, such as "Sweet Sixteen Party for Marilyn Baxter" or "Buffet dinner before the dance."

Plus information on what to wear—"blue jeans," "black tie," "bring your bathing suit."

Plus "R.s.v.p." and your telephone number, to make answering your invitation easier. If you're having a large party, you may want to put "Respond regrets only, please" instead of "R.s.v.p." * Or simply include in your message, "We'll be counting on you; let me know if you can't come."

A chart showing various ways to handle invitations appears on the following page.

---

* ***Répondez, s'il vous plaît***—French for "Please answer."

Treasure Training

Everything, from the first invitation to the last goodbye, has been preparing you to leave. Every party has a pick-up time. Someone has to clean up the mess; someone needs their space back. The bell's rung, graduation cap tossed in the air—and retrieved, of course, because you save it all. Surrounding the room is your collection, treasures lined up like questions you needed answered.

There's your daisy corsage, post-prom promises he didn't swear; what went wrong? Over there, the paeans to Hot Sweaters, Crayola-markered, you couldn't torch among the others when your obsession ended; does that mean you're a poet? Telling anecdotes about that term bored your friends—how many times a day he threw shit at you—so they stole the book from math class so you'd solve for WHY.

There's a boy at a dance, a privileged girl who's miserably snuffling her nose into his collar, burrowing to bury beneath a jugular, ruffled because he was bland and noncommittal about what happens next. There's the mixtape you made to answer—the plan, the place, and his phoned cancellation, obviously avoiding a make-out session with a girl that hadn't followed the metrics.

Now it's curfew—*come, you can't party forever*—as you're ushered out, a hand on your back, someone placing your coat and purse in your arms as you emerge into the world, bewildered by the sudden transition. When did you grow up? You're still forming patterns, still forgetting details—the condiments are put on the table with their serving spoons to the right, not the left. Right?

There's a woman cataloging lessons into the filing cabinet of your mind, a little girl crouching between the synapses, clutching her question, flinching every time the drawer bangs shut. How are you supposed to carry them both into your future?

The immense load of those years crushed your nervous system, the weight of watching and observing without acting. Your spine is a table; you ask yourself if this is the china of your dreams, these fussy, outdated, delicate heirlooms you were told all proper women collected.

And whose fault is that? You can reach into the crevices for a reason, but you had agency—you studied the etiquette books, swearing you needed the magazines to keep pace, to plan Fifteen Parties That are Easy and Fun!

The author guaranteed everything will come up roses for the girl who gives a Pink Party, where cupcakes bloom with frosting roses, pink posies center place cards, splashes of rose water lend fragrance to the punch bowl. But no one drank punch; everyone uncapped two liters of Sprite and poured Cheetos in a bowl before slumping back in front of the Nintendo. You found, later, each tiny pink rosebud you'd placed as a perfect memento of your perfect Pink Party, unnoticed.

Undeterred, you pressed on, selecting suggestions that seemed ageless, themes like "My Birthday" or "Halloween." You did everything right: invited boys, costumed yourself as Draculette rather than Igor, but they left before it was dark. They had other plans, other games—Which Witch is Which, a sheet across a doorway, just enough room for feet and ankles to be seen. A girl appears, barefoot—one girl at a time. The one who keeps the boys guessing the longest is the winner.

You know that. You were a skinny sideliner in baggy jeans, so eager to belong you pretended to be bulimic. You searched Goodwill for that retro gas-station shirt *Seventeen* counseled cool girls wore to dances, coerced your friend's brother, fashioning a fantasy—the boys being the wallweeds, the girls cutting in—that old game Tsohg, backward. Planned to subvert prettiness with the unexpected: a dustpan, a brush, Asherella untidied. But you caved, conventional in a velvet halter dress with sharp-pointed darts, untouched by neither breasts nor date.

You couldn't win cheating the game and you couldn't win playing it. What was the point of all these rules, these condescensions, these little shames if you became half-ghost/half-girl, nothing appearing in the mirror but your flaws? You transformed from a wall into a wallflower—*don't anybody move until you feel the magic*—but when a boy finally did, you realized he was drawn to the cultivation, greenhouse-grown, nothing natural.

A girl has goals. A goal has girls, generations of them, Darwinian adaptation widening smiles and tightening skirts, but they'll settle for safety, a situation. The goal is desire, to kneel in the middle of the room until he gets near the object he's to touch. No words are allowed. You leaned a half-inch forward and the books toppled off your head. Who would claim such a clumsy girl as a partner?

A game: "Man Hunt," the girls the aggressors, an all-out chase to catch a partner for dinner, the next dance. The boys walk in, eyes wide open, neatly evading your blindfolded grab. The zodiac labels you a cancer, predicting ten years from today you'll feel as unwelcome + excisable as you do now. So you are a crab, scuttling into a burrow, lugging the things you need from home to home, packing them in tight. Is it so wrong to hold onto an archaic manual, outmoded decades before you were born? Everyone seemed to insist it still had resonance.

You were supposed to be a Teen Queen, gliding through adolescence on your float, pageant-waving in the sun, throwing favors to the crowd. Why are you craning to see if there's more to come? The parade's over.

A girl is an assemblage of moments lined up on a shelf as treasured lessons, portents. The future presses you onto the porch, latching the lock of youth. Your goody bag is stuffed, so heavy you're sure you can't possibly carry it with you, but you will.

Trust me.

seventeen
she's the one!
is your school divided by race?
celeb hair
Matt LeBlanc
7 hot girl singers
aaliyah
alanis
5 hot new faces
Brad Renfro
reese witherspoon
550 guys
THE seventeen BOOK OF ETIQUETTE
AND ENTERTAINING
BY ENID A. HAUPT
10 ways to get over a crush
love
holiday loot
Hanson
the best and worst
natalie portman
love
no dating allowed
sarah michelle gellar
prom
tyra
the Leo you don't know
quiz: are you psychic?
guys
mega beauty issue
could it be love?
after the massacre
back to school fashion issue
celebs'
Drew Cinderella
fall fashion blowout
Brandy
Jewel
hollywood hot spots
Felicity

Acknowledgements

Thanks to:

Michael and the Autofocus team, for going another round with me

Jody, Lisa, and John, for your early and enduring support of this project

The reading teams and editors at *Split Lip Magazine, Storm Cellar, Gordon Square Review, Synaesthesia Magazine, apt., Atlas & Alice, the museum of americana, The Collagist, cahoodaloodaling, Gigantic Sequins, 45th Parallel, The Normal School, Florida Review,* and *Black Lily Magazine,* for giving some of these essays their first homes

My parents, Dave and Trina—I hid a lot of myself as a teen, but I hope I never hid how much I love you

My partner, Kevin, for never calling me "nice"

My daughters, Kirsten, Annike, and Britta, for ignoring the training

The queens who spent their teens with me—Kathy, Katherine, Eliza, Kelly, Andrea, Emilie, Angela, Erin, Emily C, Mary, Rachel, Katy, Crystal, Becky, and Jackie—beloved.

And finally, to Emily: this book is for you. Whether we were doing "something fun and exciting" or sitting on your parents' couch watching the Stories, those are the real treasured memories I keep lined up on a shelf.

About the Author

Kristine Langley Mahler is the author of *A Calendar Is a Snakeskin* and *Curing Season: Artifacts.* Her work has been supported by the Nebraska Arts Council and Art at Cedar Point and thrice named Notable in Best American Essays. A memoirist experimenting with the truth on the suburban prairie outside Omaha, Nebraska, Kristine is also the director of Split/Lip Press. Find more about her projects at kristinelangleymahler.com.

— also from Autofocus Books —

Duplex — Mike Nagel

XO — Sara Rauch

Until It Feels Right — Emily Costa

Cleave — Holly Pelesky

Nextdoor in Colonialtown — Ryan Rivas

Too Much Tongue — Adrienne Marie Barrios & Leigh Chadwick

Picture Window — Danny Caine

the nature machine! — Tyler Gillespie

A Kind of In-Between — Aaron Burch

How to Write a Novel: An Anthology of 20 Craft Essays About Writing, None of Which Ever Mention Writing — ed. Aaron Burch

Hiraeth — Mistie R. Watkins

That Spell — Tate N. Oquendo

My Modest Blindness — Russell Brakefield

A Calendar Is A Snakeskin — Kristine Langley Mahler

Culdesac — Mike Nagel

Razed by TV Sets — Jason McCall

In the Away Time — Kristen E. Nelson

The Body Is A Temporary Gathering Place — Andrew Bertaina

Daughterhood — Emily Adrian

A Healthy Interest in the Lives of Others — Teresa Carmody

Yes I Am Human I Know You Were Wondering — Erin Dorney

Leave: A Postpartum Account — Shayne Terry

Out There In the Dark — Katharine Coldiron

If I Can Be Honest: Selected Prose from the Four Years of Autofocus Lit (2020-2024) — ed. Michael Wheaton

The Dead Dad Diaries — Erin Slaughter

A Revionist History of Loving Men — Lena Ziegler

Marginalia — Naomi Washer

The Third Beat — Lauren Lavín

Tacoma — Aaron Burch